ブルース・リーの霊言
ドラゴンの復活

大川隆法
RYUHO OKAWA

本霊言は、2017年8月13日、幸福の科学 特別説法堂にて、
公開収録された(写真上・下)。

ブルース・リーの霊言
──ドラゴンの復活──

Spiritual Interview with Bruce Lee

Preface

Now, here, he is. Famous "Dragon" came back. Who was he? What was he? And, now, where, why, how he is? Is it be possible for him to be a dragon, even after his death? I mean "kung fu" or "Jeet Kune Do" can be understood in the realm of spirits, that is, without bodies.

In this book, Bruce Lee talked a lot about his philosophy. How could he use the word, "Fighting" compatible with "Peaceful Philosophy"?

Can "kung fu" be replaced by the words "Justice" "Love" "Peace" "Way" or "Buddha's Truth"?

Anyway, you can see "The Resurrection of the Dragon" in this book. And this fact will be the good news for the people of the world who still respecting Bruce Lee.

Nov. 10, 2017

Master, Founder & CEO of Happy Science Group

Ryuho Okawa

はじめに

　今、ここに、彼はいる。有名な「ドラゴン」が帰って
きた。彼って誰? 彼って何? そして、今、ここで、なぜ、
彼が出てくるんだ。死んだ後でもドラゴンのままでいら
れるって? つまり、「カンフー」や「ジークンドー(截拳
道)」は、霊界でも、えー、肉体がなくなってからも、他
の人たち(霊たち)に通じるのかな。

　この本では、ブルース・リーは彼の哲学をまくしたてて
いる。どうやって彼は「武闘」を「平和哲学」と言いくる
めたか。「カンフー」が「正義」や「愛」「平安」「道」さ
らには「仏法真理」と言いかえられるのだろうか。

　言葉の詮索はともかく、この本を読み進めれば、「ドラ
ゴンの復活」を目のあたりにすることは受け合いだ。その
事実が、世界中にいるブルース・リーの信奉者たちへの福
音となるだろう。

2017 年 11 月 10 日
悟りたる者にして幸福の科学グループの創始者兼総裁
大川隆法

Contents

Preface 2

1 A Worldwide Star of Oriental Origin
Returns After 44 Years 14

The riddle of his early death and his whereabouts
in the other world 14

He is an Oriental hero, even now 20

Bruce Lee appears, showing off his moves 26

"I am still fighting" 34

"My spirit is my body and my body is my spirit" 46

2 Truth, Beauty, and Justice According to
Bruce Lee 54

The spirit of Jeet Kune Do is the pursuit of the Truth 54

Jeet Kune Do is "the world's most beautiful and strongest
martial art" 64

On the strength, confidence, and justice of martial artists 76

3 Taoism and Freedom Believed by Bruce Lee 82

Asian people can conquer their inferiority complex toward
white people by training 82

Taoism is the Truth of the world 86

"I believe in God" 94

Bruce Lee speaks about harmony and energy of the universe 98

目　次

はじめに ……………………………………………………… 3

1　東洋発の世界的スター、死後44年ぶりの復活 ……… 15

「早すぎた死」の謎とあの世の行き先は ……………… 15

今も色褪せぬ東洋のヒーロー ……………………… 21

登場と同時にアクション全開 ……………………… 27

「私はずっと戦っている」 ……………………………… 35

「霊即肉体、肉体即霊」 ……………………………… 47

2　ブルース・リーが語る「真理、美、正義」 …………… 55

截拳道の精神は「真理の探究」 ……………………… 55

截拳道は「世界一、美しくて強い武術」 ……………… 65

武術家の「強さ、自信、正義」について ……………… 77

3　ブルース・リーが信じる「タオイズムと自由」 ……… 83

アジア人は鍛錬の力で白人への劣等感に克てる ……… 83

タオイズム（道教）こそ世界の真理 ………………… 87

「私は神を信じている」 ……………………………… 95

宇宙の調和とエネルギーを語る ……………………… 99

Freedom means to be free from physical bondage 104

4 China, Japan, and North Korea as Analyzed by Bruce Lee 110

Bruce Lee spread the Chinese spirit to the world through kung fu 110

Movies are a new weapon 118

The Communist Party of China will collapse within 10 years.. 120

There will be another hero after Liu Xiaobo 134

North Korea should ask Japan to rescue them 138

5 Bruce Lee Reveals His Past Life, the Truth of His Death, and the Mission of His Soul 146

"I was a dragon in every time" 146

The spiritual truth of his early death 156

Bruce Lee's mission as a destroyer of the old age 160

After the spiritual interview 170

* This spiritual interview was conducted in English. The Japanese text is a translation added by the Happy Science International Editorial Division.

自由とは「肉体の束縛からの解放」 ……………………………… 105

4 ブルース・リーが分析する「中国、日本、北朝鮮」 …… 111

カンフーで世界に中国精神を広めた ……………………………… 111

映画は「新たな武器」である ……………………………………… 119

中国共産党は 10 年以内に崩壊する ……………………………… 121

劉暁波のあとに「次なるヒーロー」が出る ……………………… 135

北朝鮮は日本に救いを求めよ ……………………………………… 139

5 ブルース・リーが明かす「過去世、死の真相、

魂の使命」 …………………………………………………………… 147

私はいつの時代も「ドラゴン」だった ………………………… 147

「早すぎた死」のスピリチュアルな真相 ……………………… 157

古い時代の破壊者としての使命 ………………………………… 161

霊言を終えて ……………………………………………………… 171

※本書は、英語で収録された霊言に和訳を付けたものです。

This book is the transcript of spiritual messages given by Bruce Lee.

These spiritual messages were channeled through Ryuho Okawa. However, please note that because of his high level of enlightenment, his way of receiving spiritual messages is fundamentally different from other psychic mediums who undergo trances and are completely taken over by the spirits they are channeling.

It should be noted that these spiritual messages are opinions of the individual spirits and may contradict the ideas or teachings of the Happy Science Group.

本書は、ブルース・リーの霊言を収録したものである。

　「霊言現象」とは、あの世の霊存在の言葉を語り下ろす現象のことをいう。これは高度な悟りを開いた者に特有のものであり、「霊媒現象」（トランス状態になって意識を失い、霊が一方的にしゃべる現象）とは異なる。

　ただ、「霊言」は、あくまでも霊人の意見であり、幸福の科学グループとしての見解と矛盾する内容を含む場合がある点、付記しておきたい。

Spiritual Interview with Bruce Lee

August 13, 2017 at Special Lecture Hall, Happy Science
Spiritual Interview with Bruce Lee

ブルース・リーの霊言

── ドラゴンの復活 ──

2017 年 8 月 13 日　幸福の科学 特別説法堂にて
ブルース・リーの霊言

Bruce Lee (1940-1973)

A martial artist and movie actor. His father was an actor in Hong Kong and was on tour in San Francisco, U.S. where Bruce Lee was born. Once returning to Hong Kong, he became a child actor in Hong Kong movies by the stage name Li Xiaolong. He became fixated on martial arts and while enrolled at the University of Washington, he created his own original form of martial art, Jeet Kune Do. His fighting skills attracted Hollywood's attention and he became an action star in American TV shows. In 1971, he returned to Hong Kong to act in the movie, *The Big Boss*. Afterward, he achieved his dream of acting in a Hollywood movie by starring in *Enter the Dragon*. However, he was bothered by severe headaches for an unknown reason and, in July 1973, right before the release of his movie, suddenly passed away. *Enter the Dragon* was a huge hit, and he became a worldwide star after his death.

Interviewers from Happy Science

Masayuki Isono
Executive Director
Chief of Overseas Missionary Work Promotion Office
Deputy Chief Secretary, First Secretarial Division
Religious Affairs Headquarters

Taishu Sakai
Special Assistant to the Chairperson
Religious Affairs Headquarters

Yuki Wada
General Manager, First Secretarial Division,
General Manager of Overseas Missionary Work Promotion
Office, Religious Affairs Headquarters

※ Interviewers are listed in the order that they appear in the transcript.
The professional titles are the position at the time of the interview.

ブルース・リー（1940－1973）

武術家。映画俳優。父は香港の俳優で、巡業先だった米国サンフランシスコで生まれる。香港に戻り、李小龍という芸名で、幼少時から香港映画に出演。また、武術に熱中し、ワシントン大学在学中、截拳道という独自の武術を創始する。彼の武術はハリウッドから注目され、アクション俳優として米国のテレビドラマに出演するようになる。1971年、香港に戻り、香港映画「ドラゴン危機一発」に主演。その後、念願だったハリウッド映画への進出を果たし、「燃えよドラゴン」に主演する。ところが、原因不明の激しい頭痛にたびたび襲われるようになり、映画公開直前の73年7月、急死。「燃えよドラゴン」は大ヒットし、死して世界のスターとなった。

質問者（幸福の科学）

磯野将之 　（理事 兼 宗務本部海外伝道推進室長 兼
　　　　　　　第一秘書局担当局長）

酒井太守 　（宗務本部担当理事長特別補佐）

和田ゆき 　（宗務本部第一秘書局部長 兼
　　　　　　　海外伝道推進室部長）

※質問順。役職は収録当時のもの。

1 A Worldwide Star of Oriental Origin Returns After 44 Years

The riddle of his early death and his whereabouts in the other world

Ryuho Okawa Hello. We would like to summon the spirit of the famous Bruce Lee, the kung fu movie actor.

He is still famous worldwide. I knew him in my high school days, and he died in 1973. But after his death, he became famous through his movies. Even in Japan, a lot of his followers still respect him, especially people who are directing kung fu, martial arts or karate-like area, and actors and actresses. These people have deep, deep respect for him.

So today, we must investigate how he has been in the afterlife or spiritual world. When I wrote *The Mystical Laws*,* I wrote that the famous Bruce Lee might

---

* See Chapter Four in *The Mystical Laws* (New York: IRH Press, 2015).

1 東洋発の世界的スター、死後44年ぶりの復活

「早すぎた死」の謎とあの世の行き先は

大川隆法　こんにちは。有名なカンフー映画俳優のブルース・リーの霊を呼んでみたいと思います。

　彼は今でも世界的に有名です。私が彼を知ったのは高校時代で、1973年に亡くなりましたが、亡くなってから映画を通して有名になりました。日本でも多くのファンが今も彼を尊敬しておりますし、特にカンフー、武術、空手などの指導にあたっている人たちや、俳優や女優などから、非常に深く尊敬されています。

　そこで今日は、彼が現在まで、死後の世界、霊界でどうなっているのかを調べてみないといけません。『神秘の法』（注）には、「有名なブルース・リーは、死後、幽霊

(注)　『神秘の法』（大川隆法著・幸福の科学出版刊）第4章参照。

15

have dropped into not the heavenly world because I've heard from people that after his death, he appeared as a ghost and they said at that time, he smelled bad. In the context of Chinese tradition, how good they smell is very essential. When they smell bad, it means the person is in Hell. But today, we are living in 2017, 44 years from his death. So, is his situation the same or not? We cannot be sure about it, so we want to check it.

But firstly, I must apologize to you. I cannot show the action of Bruce Lee in front of you because of my poor action now. So, it's difficult for me. It would mean my death, so I cannot.

Today's purpose is, we want to know the spirit of Jeet Kune Do. The founder is Bruce Lee. So, he has a philosophy regarding kung fu, especially *his* kung fu. Firstly, he was the disciple of famous Ip Man*, the grand master of Eishunken (Wing Chun) sector.

---

* Ip Man (1893~1972) A master of Wing Chun. Born in Guangdong Province, China. He mastered Wing Chun, a traditional martial art in southern China. He spread Wing Chun in Hong Kong after WWII and developed his branch of Wing Chun, making it the largest in Hong Kong.

として出てきて、そのとき悪臭が漂ったと言われているので、天上界ではない世界に堕ちたのかもしれない」と書きました。中国の伝統では、どんな匂いがしたかということが極めて重要で、悪臭がした場合は、その人が地獄に堕ちていることを意味するのですが、現在は2017年で、彼の死後44年が経過しており、同じ状況かどうか定かではありませんので、確かめてみたいと思います。

　ただ、最初に謝っておかなければいけませんが、私は現在、アクションが得意ではありませんので、皆さんの前でブルース・リーのアクションをお見せすることはできません。難しくて死んでしまいますので、私にはできません。

　今日の目的としては、ブルース・リーが創始者である「截拳道」の精神に迫ってみたいということです。この方には、カンフーに関する、特に自らのカンフーに関する哲学があります。最初は詠春拳のグランド・マスター（宗師）である有名なイップ・マン（葉問・注）の弟子で

（注）葉問（英語名イップ・マン）（1893〜1972）詠春拳の達人。中国・広東省に生まれ、中国南部に伝わる伝統武術・詠春拳を習得。第二次大戦後、香港に移り詠春拳を広め、葉問派詠春拳を香港で最も有力な流派へと発展させた。

1 A Worldwide Star of Oriental Origin Returns After 44 Years

Ip Man is very famous. Ip Man is Bruce Lee's *shifu* (fatherly master), but he was poor at making money and making the name of Eishunken prevail. Contrary to that, Bruce Lee was very good at making money (especially after this death) and he became famous in the world. So, through his famous movies, he became the hero of the movie world.

Here, I have several movies, for example, *The Big Boss*; this one is *Dragon Kiki Ippatsu* in Japanese [*laughs*].

From left to right: *The Big Boss* (Golden Harvest, 1971), *Fist of Fury* (ibid, 1972), *The Way of the Dragon* (ibid, 1972)
左から「ドラゴン危機一発」（1971年公開／パラマウント ホーム エンタテインメント ジャパン）「ドラゴン怒りの鉄拳」（1972年公開／同）「ドラゴンへの道」（1972年公開／同）

18

した。イップ・マンは非常に有名な方で、ブルース・リーの師父でしたが、この方はお金儲けや詠春拳の名を広めることは下手でした。ブルース・リーのほうはお金儲けがたいへん上手で（特に死後）、世界的に有名になりました。有名な出演作を通して映画界のヒーローになった方です。

ここに何本か映画を持ってきましたが、たとえば「ザ・ビッグ・ボス」、日本語では「ドラゴン危機一発」です（笑）。

Game of Death (ibid, 1978), *The Tower of Death* (ibid, 1981), *Enter the Dragon* (ibid, 1973)
「死亡遊戯」（1978年公開／同）「死亡の塔」（1981年公開／同）「燃えよドラゴン」（1973年公開／ワーナー・ホーム・ビデオ）

Fist of Fury, or *Dragon Ikari no Tekken* [*laughs*], *The Way of the Dragon*, or *Doragon e no Michi*, *Game of Death*, or *Shibo Yugi*, and *Tower of Death*, or *Shibo no Tou*.

Young people are not familiar with Bruce Lee. [*While showing the Blu-ray disc cases*] This is his face, what he looks like. I'm sorry I cannot show you something. If I'm Dragon Li Xiaolong, I can kick the ceiling of this room [*laughs*], (but I'm not,) so I'm very sorry about that.

He is an Oriental hero, even now

Ryuho Okawa OK. Is it enough on him? OK, OK, OK. I'll add an additional one.

He learned kung fu, but his original Jeet Kune Do is quite different. Its concept is made up from a lot of martial arts, Judo, boxing or things like that. So, the form of Jeet Kune Do is quite contrary to that of common kung fu. His shifu, Ip Man, taught him Eishunken. It's some kind of defensive-type kung fu.

「ドラゴン怒りの鉄拳」（笑）、「ドラゴンへの道」、「死亡遊戯」そして「死亡の塔」ですね。

　若い人はブルース・リーに馴染みがないでしょうが、（ブルーレイディスクのジャケットを示しながら）こういう顔の人です。こういう外見です。残念ながらお見せできないものもありまして。私がドラゴン李小龍（ブルース・リーの中国語芸名）なら、この部屋の天井をキックできるのですが（笑）、その点は、たいへん申し訳ないと思っています。

今も色褪せぬ東洋のヒーロー

大川隆法　オーケー、彼についての説明としては十分でしょうか。そうそう、付け加えることがありました。

　彼はカンフーを学びましたが、彼のオリジナルである截拳道はかなり違っていて、そのコンセプトは多くの武術や柔道、ボクシングなどから成り立っています。截拳道の型は、普通のカンフーとは逆です。師父のイップ・マンが彼に教えたのは詠春拳で、こちらは一種の「防御型カンフー」ですが、彼の截拳道は「攻撃型」であると思います。キッ

But his Jeet Kune Do is an aggressive one. I think so. It seems like kickboxing or something like that.

He became famous through his movies, but to our regret, he died at the age of 32. He died too young. After his death, maybe *Moeyo Doragon* [*Enter the Dragon*] became famous in the world and he became a worldwide star. Before that, he appeared in the U.S. TV series, *Green Hornet*, as a karate actor for a character with a Japanese name, Kato, and became a great star.

His death is a riddle now. After his death, several movies regarding his life story were made, and even now, people know his famous, how do I say, dragon-bird-like voice, "Acho! Acho!" or [*laughs*] his nunchaku, so he really is the origin of the kung fu movie stars. We now have Jackie Chan, Jet Li or people like that, but he's the first one of the Oriental superstars, and was and is a hero of the Oriental world. I think so.

Then, I'll summon Bruce Lee.

He was born in the U.S.A., and of course, he had citizenship of the United States. But before the age of

クボクシングか何かのようにも見えます。

　彼は映画で有名になりましたが、惜しくも32歳で亡くなりました。早すぎる死でした。亡くなってから「燃えよドラゴン」が世界的に有名になり、世界的スターになったのだと思います。それ以前には、アメリカの「グリーン・ホーネット」というテレビシリーズに、カトーという日本人名の役で空手俳優として出演し、大スターになっていました。

　この方の死は、今も謎に包まれています。死後、彼の人生に関する映画が何本か作られており、現在でも、あの有名な「アチョー！アチョー！」という、（英語では）何と言うか、「怪鳥音」や（笑）ヌンチャクで知られています。ですから、まさにカンフー映画スターの元祖です。今はジャッキー・チェンやジェット・リーなどもいますが、彼が最初の東洋のスーパースターであり、昔も今も東洋世界のヒーローであると言えるでしょう。

　それでは、ブルース・リーをお呼びしたいと思います。

　この方はアメリカ生まれですので、当然アメリカ市民権があったのですが、1歳になる前に香港に戻っていま

one, he returned to Hong Kong and in his younger days, he acted as a small movie star because his father was an actor of Hong Kong. After he became 19 years old, he entered the University of Washington and majored in philosophy, so his Jeet Kune Do kung fu has a philosophical aspect. He has pride in that aspect. So today, we must ask him about his philosophy and what he thinks of China, Hong Kong, Japan, or the U.S.A. This is today's subject. I think so.

I'm not sure if he can speak Japanese or not, but firstly, we'll start in English and then we can pursue his past life. Is it OK?

OK, then, famous actor Bruce Lee.

Would you come down here to Happy Science?

I am very sorry for making you wait three weeks.

You came to me

Before the Tokyo Dome lecture[*],

---

[*] The author gave a grand lecture entitled "The Choice of Humankind" at Tokyo Dome on August 2, 2017.

す。父親が香港の俳優でしたので、彼も幼少時は子役で映画に出ていました。19歳でワシントン大学に入学して哲学を専攻しています。ですから、彼の截拳道カンフーには哲学的側面があり、その点を誇りに思っているようです。そこで今日は、彼の哲学や、中国や香港、あるいは日本やアメリカに関する考えを聞いてみないといけません。それが今日のテーマになるかと思います。

　日本語を話せるかどうかわかりませんが、最初は英語で始めてみて、そこから過去世を追跡してみたいと思います。よろしいでしょうか。

　それでは、名優ブルース・リーよ
　ここ、幸福の科学にご降臨いただけますでしょうか。
　3週間もお待たせしてしまい、申し訳ありません。
　東京ドームの大講演会（注）の前に
　私のところに来られましたが

（注）2017年8月2日、東京ドームにて特別大講演会「人類の選択」を行った。

But I let you wait more than three weeks.

I'm very sorry.

Would you please speak something for us?

[*About 10 seconds of silence.*]

Bruce Lee appears, showing off his moves

Bruce Lee [*Suddenly thrusts right hand forward, turns sideways and sticks up left index finger next to face, as if taking a Jeet Kune Do stance.*] Tou!!

Masayuki Isono Hello?

３週間以上もお待たせしてしまいました。

たいへん申し訳ございません。

われらのために、何かお話しいただけますでしょうか。

（約10秒間の沈黙）

登場と同時にアクション全開

ブルース・リー　（突然、截拳道の構えのように右手を前に突き出して半身になり、人差し指を上げた左手を顔の横に引きつけて）トゥ──!!

磯野将之　こんにちは。

Bruce Lee attracted fans worldwide with his powerful kung fu moves (a scene from *Enter the Dragon*).
迫力あるカンフーで、世界の人々を魅了したブルース・リー（映画「燃えよドラゴン」より）。

1 A Worldwide Star of Oriental Origin Returns After 44 Years

Bruce Lee Acho!

[*Interviewers laugh.*]

Bruce Lee [*While slowly making various hand movements.*] Oooh... Ko!

Isono Hello.

Bruce Lee Huh… Hello!

Isono Are you Mr. Bruce Lee?

Bruce Lee Sure. [*Performs a move.*] Ch! Chowaa...

Isono [*Laughs.*] Thank you for coming to Happy Science.

Bruce Lee What's Happy Science?

ブルース・リー　アチョー！

（質問者　笑）

ブルース・リー　（両手を様々にゆっくり動かしながら）
オゥオオオォォォォ……コッ！

磯野　こんにちは。

ブルース・リー　ハ……ハロー！

磯野　ブルース・リーさんでいらっしゃいますでしょうか。

ブルース・リー　そうです。　（アクションをしながら）
チッ！　チョウワァァァ……。

磯野　（笑）幸福の科学にお越しくださり、ありがとうご
ざいます。

ブルース・リー　幸福の科学とは何だ。

Isono "What's Happy Science?" We will explain it later, but…

Bruce Lee [*Shows many stances as if in an action scene, and takes a pose in the end.*]

Isono [*Laughs.*] Thank you. We are so happy to have you here.

Bruce Lee Uh-huh.

Isono We'd like to ask you several questions about your life in the other world.

Bruce Lee Uh-huh.

Isono And… [*Watches Bruce Lee act out Jeet Kune Do and nunchaku moves in his chair, but continues asking despite being interrupted.*]… about the philosophy of your… Jeet Kune Do and… current world issues.

1 東洋発の世界的スター、死後44年ぶりの復活

磯野　幸福の科学が何であるかは後ほど説明いたします
が……。

ブルース・リー　（流れるようにいろいろなアクションの
構えをし、最後に決めポーズ）

磯野　（笑）ありがとうございます。お迎えすることができ
き、たいへん嬉しく思います。

ブルース・リー　うん。

磯野　あなたの、あの世での生活についていくつかご質
問させていただきます。

ブルース・リー　うん。

磯野　また……（ブルース・リーが、椅子に座ったまま
盛んに、截拳道の動きや、ヌンチャクを扱うようなアク
ションをする様子を見て、間合いを見ながら切れ切れに
言葉を続ける）あなたの……截拳道哲学や……現在の世

31

Bruce Lee [*Preoccupied with his moves, he misses Isono's words*] Uh-huh. What?

Isono Sorry.

Bruce Lee What?

Isono We would like to ask you several questions.

Bruce Lee Several questions?

Isono Please teach us your philo...

Bruce Lee Teach you? What?

Isono Your thinking.

Bruce Lee Thinking?

界の問題についても。

ブルース・リー　（アクションに没頭していて質問者の言葉を聞いていなかった）ん、何？

磯野　すみません。

ブルース・リー　何だって？

磯野　いくつか質問させていただきます。

ブルース・リー　質問？

磯野　教えていただきたいのですが。あなたの哲……。

ブルース・リー　教える？　何を？

磯野　あなたのお考えです。

ブルース・リー　考え？

Isono Yes.

Bruce Lee I'm thinking, yeah.

"I am still fighting"

Isono OK, so first of all, as Master Okawa explained earlier, just after you died, your ghost appeared and the smell was terribly bad. People used to say that you might have fallen down to Hell.

Bruce Lee [*Shuffling and looking at the Blu-ray disc cases of the movies starring himself.*] Hmm? Hell? No, no.

Isono Was it true?

Bruce Lee No! No, no, no.

Isono No, no?

磯野　はい。

ブルース・リー　ああ、考えてますよ。

「私はずっと戦っている」

磯野　はい。では初めに、大川総裁が先ほど説明されましたように、あなたがお亡くなりになった直後、あなたの幽霊が現れて、ひどい悪臭がしましたので、あなたは地獄に堕ちたのかもしれないと言われていました。

ブルース・リー　（自分の出演映画のブルーレイディスクを次々に手に取り、ジャケットを眺めながら）ん？ 地獄？いやいや。

磯野　それは本当でしょうか。

ブルース・リー　違う！　違う、違う、違う。

磯野　違いますか。

Bruce Lee No. Completely no.

Isono So…

Bruce Lee [*Imitates the pose on the Blu-ray disc cover.*] Cho!

Isono [*Laughs.*] Where were you at that time?

Bruce Lee Hmm?

Isono Where were you right after you died?

Bruce Lee I'm fighting.

Isono You are fighting?

Bruce Lee Still fighting.

Isono You're still fighting?

ブルース・リー　違う。まったく違う。

磯野　では……。

ブルース・リー　（ブルーレイディスクを見ながら、ジャケット写真の自分のポーズを真似して）チョオ！

磯野　（笑）そのとき、どこにいらしたのですか。

ブルース・リー　うん？

磯野　亡くなられた直後は、どこにいらしたのですか。

ブルース・リー　戦ってるんです。

磯野　戦っている？

ブルース・リー　ずっと戦ってる。

磯野　ずっと戦っていると。

Bruce Lee Hmm.

Taishu Sakai Where do you live now?

Bruce Lee Hmm?

Sakai Live now?

Bruce Lee Hmm?

Sakai Where do you live now?

Bruce Lee Here.

Isono Here? Where? Where is "here"?

Bruce Lee Here.

Isono No, no, no.

1　東洋発の世界的スター、死後44年ぶりの復活

ブルース・リー　うん。

酒井太守　現在はどこに住んでいらっしゃるのでしょうか。

ブルース・リー　うん？

酒井　現在はどこにお住まいですか。

ブルース・リー　んー？

酒井　現在はどこに住んでいらっしゃいますか。

ブルース・リー　ここです。

磯野　ここ？　どこですか。「ここ」とはどこでしょうか。

ブルース・リー　ここ。

磯野　いえいえいえ。

39

Bruce Lee In front of you.

Isono No. Yes, we can see you, but you are now a spirit, so…

Bruce Lee [*Grunts as he shows his moves.*] Ho!

Isono OK, do you understand that you don't have a body of yours?

Bruce Lee No.

Isono No?

Bruce Lee No. I have a body with me.

Isono What kind of body do you have?

Bruce Lee Beautiful body.

1　東洋発の世界的スター、死後44年ぶりの復活

ブルース・リー　君たちの目の前。

磯野　いえ。はい、あなたがいらっしゃるのは見えますが、現在は霊でいらっしゃるので……。

ブルース・リー　んんんー（アクションをしながら）ホッ！

磯野　はい。ご自分にはもう肉体がないことは、おわかりですか。

ブルース・リー　いや。

磯野　わからない？

ブルース・リー　いや。肉体はあります。

磯野　どんな肉体ですか。

ブルース・リー　美しい肉体がある。

41

1 A Worldwide Star of Oriental Origin Returns After 44 Years

Isono Beautiful body?

Bruce Lee Can I take off? [*Tries to take off jacket.*]

Isono No, no, no. Please don't, please don't.

Bruce Lee Oh. [*Sits back with a relaxed expression.*]

Yuki Wada Who are you fighting?

Bruce Lee Hmm?

Wada Who are you fighting?

Bruce Lee Enemy.

Wada Who is your enemy?

磯野　美しい肉体？

ブルース・リー　脱いでもいいかな（ジャケットを脱ぎ
かける動作）。

磯野　いえいえいえ。やめてください、やめてください。

ブルース・リー　オウ（リラックスした表情で身を引き、
ゆったりと椅子に座る）。

和田ゆき　誰と戦っているのですか。

ブルース・リー　うん？

和田　誰と戦っているのですか。

ブルース・リー　敵ですよ。

和田　敵とは誰ですか。

1 A Worldwide Star of Oriental Origin Returns After 44 Years

Bruce Lee Devils. Devils, devils. Worldwide devils. Bad people of the world.

Isono Bad people? For example?

Bruce Lee Hmm? Mafia, gang, American racists, or Chinese evil politicians, like that.

Isono Evil politicians?

Bruce Lee [*Takes a Jeet Kune Do stance.*] Ocho! Ah…

Isono So, you are still in this world and fighting that kind of evil people?

Bruce Lee Are you good people?

Isono Yes, we are.

1　東洋発の世界的スター、死後44年ぶりの復活

ブルース・リー　悪魔ですよ、悪魔。悪魔。世界的な悪魔。世界中の悪人ども。

磯野　悪人とは、たとえば？

ブルース・リー　ん？　マフィアとかギャングとか、アメリカの人種差別主義者とか、中国の悪徳政治家とか、そういう奴らです。

磯野　悪徳政治家ですか。

ブルース・リー　（截拳道の構えで）オチョー！　アー……。

磯野　すると、まだこの世で、そういう悪人たちと戦っていらっしゃるのですか。

ブルース・リー　君たちは善人かな。

磯野　はい、そうです。

45

Bruce Lee [*Points to Sakai.*] He is questionable.

Sakai Good people, good people.

Bruce Lee Really?

Sakai Yes.

"My spirit is my body and my body is my spirit"

Bruce Lee Oh! Hmm… Hmm… OK. Oh, [*points to Wada*] you, beautiful lady.

Wada Hello.

Bruce Lee Oh, Chinese? Or…?

Wada My father is from Hong Kong.

ブルース・リー　（酒井を指して）彼は怪しいね。

酒井　善人です、善人です。

ブルース・リー　本当かな。

酒井　はい。

「霊即肉体、肉体即霊」

ブルース・リー　オー！　うん……うん……。オーケー。ああ、（和田を指して）君、美人だね。

和田　こんにちは。

ブルース・リー　おお、中国人か、それとも……。

和田　父が香港出身なんです。

Bruce Lee Hong Kong! Oh, yeah, good place.

Wada He practices aikido and has a black belt.

Bruce Lee Oh, really?

Wada So, he is a big fan of yours.

Bruce Lee [*Takes a fighting pose.*] Down! I want to fight him.

Wada I think my father would lose against you. Actually, he is a very big fan. And… [*Bruce Lee stands up and throws a kick toward Isono with right leg.*] I think you are going to hurt yourself, so please sit down [*laughs*].

Bruce Lee OK.

Sakai Why did you come?

ブルース・リー　香港！　ああ、いいところだよね。

和田　父は合気道をやっていまして、黒帯の有段者です。

ブルース・リー　おお、そうですか。

和田　ですから、父はブルース・リーさんの大ファンなんです。

ブルース・リー　（ファイティングポーズで）倒す！　勝負してみたいね。

和田　あなたにはかないません。本当にあなたの大ファンなんですよ。それと……（ブルース・リー、立ち上がり磯野のほうに向かって右キック）お怪我をなさるといけないですから、お座りください（笑）。

ブルース・リー　オーケー。

酒井　なぜ、いらしたのですか。

Bruce Lee Naked is beautiful [*gesturing his urge to take off jacket*].

Wada The jacket you have on right now is beautiful.

Sakai Why did you come to our Master?

Bruce Lee Your Master?

Sakai Why?

Bruce Lee Ryuho Okawa is a kung fu master, so…

Sakai Kung fu master?

Bruce Lee I came here to fight with him. Ha! Grand master champion.

1　東洋発の世界的スター、死後44年ぶりの復活

ブルース・リー　裸(はだか)は美しいんだよ（ジャケットを脱ぎたそうな動作）。

和田　今着ていらっしゃるジャケットは素敵ですね。

酒井　なぜ、総裁（マスター）のところにいらしたのですか。

ブルース・リー　マスター？

酒井　なぜですか。

ブルース・リー　大川隆法はカンフー・マスターだから……。

酒井　カンフー・マスター？

ブルース・リー　彼と戦うために来た。ハッ！ グランド・マスター・チャンピオンと。

51

1 A Worldwide Star of Oriental Origin Returns After 44 Years

Sakai Do you understand that you are a spirit?

Bruce Lee Yeah. I'm a spirit and I have a body.

Sakai You have a body, even now?

Bruce Lee My spirit is my body. My body is my spirit. You know?

Sakai Yeah.

Isono Yes.

Bruce Lee My spirit is beautiful. My body is beautiful. Beauty… is myself.

酒井　ご自分が霊であることは、おわかりですか。

ブルース・リー　ああ。霊だけど、肉体はある。

酒井　今でも肉体があるんですか。

ブルース・リー　私の場合は、「霊即肉体、肉体即霊」なんです。わかる？

酒井　ええ。

磯野　はい。

ブルース・リー　私のスピリット（霊、精神）は美しく、肉体も美しい。美とは……私自身です。

2 Truth, Beauty, and Justice According to Bruce Lee

The spirit of Jeet Kune Do is the pursuit of the Truth

Isono OK. I'd like to ask about the spirit of Jeet Kune Do.

Bruce Lee [*Preoccupied with his moves, he misses Isono's words.*] Hmm?

Isono The spirit of Jeet Kune Do.

Bruce Lee Oh! The spirit of Jeet Kune Do is the pursuit of the Truth. You're also pursuing the Truth, Goodness, and Beauty. Me, too. Jeet Kune Do, too. All.

2 ブルース・リーが語る「真理、美、正義」

截拳道の精神は「真理の探究」

磯野　わかりました。截拳道の精神について伺いたいと思います。

ブルース・リー　（アクションをしていて聞いていなかった）ん？

磯野　截拳道の精神です。

ブルース・リー　ああ！ 截拳道の精神は、真理の探究です。君たちも「真・善・美」を探究してるし……私もですよ。截拳道も、そう。すべて。

55

Isono OK. You often used to say that your motto is, "Honestly express yourself." So, my question is…

Bruce Lee [*While performing some moves.*] OK.

Isono Who are you? What are you?

Bruce Lee What? Hmm? Are you OK? Are you OK?

Isono Yes, I am OK.

Bruce Lee Do you have a problem in your brain?

Isono No, not at all.

Bruce Lee Oh, then it's OK.

Isono I asked because you said "to express yourself

磯野　なるほど。あなたはよく、「自分を正直に表現せよ」というのがモットーだとおっしゃっていました。そこでお聞きしたいのですが……。

ブルース・リー　（アクションをしながら）オーケー。

磯野　あなたはどなたなのでしょうか。あなたは何者なのでしょうか。

ブルース・リー　何？ ん？ 君、大丈夫か。大丈夫？

磯野　はい、大丈夫です。

ブルース・リー　頭がおかしいんじゃないの。

磯野　いえ、全然。

ブルース・リー　ああ、ならいいけど。

磯野　あなたが、「自己表現こそ、自分の精神であり、截

is your spirit or spirit of Jeet Kune Do." That's why I asked you, "Who do you think you are?" or "Who are you?"

Bruce Lee "Who are you?" It's a Zen mondo-like [Zen dialogue-like] question.

Isono Yeah, it's kind of like Zen-mondo, but you are a seeker of the Truth, so maybe you have an answer?

Bruce Lee Yeah. [*Stands up and does a squat and other moves, and speaks in a deep voice.*] I am here. [*While throwing karate punches.*] I am. I am!

[*Interviewers laugh.*]

Wada Please take a seat.

Bruce Lee [*Remains standing and extends right fist.*] This fist is the Truth! You know?

拳道の精神とも言える」とおっしゃっていたからです。ですから、あなたが自分を誰だと思っているか、あなたは誰であるのかをお尋ねしているわけです。

ブルース・リー 「あなたは誰か」って、〝禅問答〟みたいな質問だね。

磯野 はい、ある種の禅問答ですが、あなたは真理の求道者（どうしゃ）であり、答えをお持ちかと思うのですが。

ブルース・リー ああ（立ち上がってスクワットなどのアクションをしながら、低い声で）。我（われ）、ここにあり。（正拳突きをしながら）我あり。我あり！

（質問者 笑）

和田 お座りください。

ブルース・リー （立ったまま右の拳（こぶし）を出して）この拳が真理である！ わかるかな？

59

Isono The fist is the Truth?

Bruce Lee [*While performing some moves.*] Cho, cho! Acho! [*Sits on the chair.*] You know? Ah, this is the Truth.

Isono Umm... [*Laughs.*] Could you explain it in words please?

Bruce Lee [*Waves right hand to express denial.*]

Isono No?

Bruce Lee There is no word.

Isono There is no word?

Bruce Lee The Truth is... empty.

Isono Empty?

2 ブルース・リーが語る「真理、美、正義」

磯野　その拳が真理なのですか。

ブルース・リー　（アクション）チョー、チョー！ アチョー！（椅子に座り）わかる？ うん、これが真理なんだよ。

磯野　えー……（笑）。言葉で表現していただけませんでしょうか。

ブルース・リー　（右手を横に振って否定の動作）

磯野　駄目ですか。

ブルース・リー　言葉はない。

磯野　言葉はないと。

ブルース・リー　真理とは……「空」である。

磯野　空ですか。

2 Truth, Beauty, and Justice According to Bruce Lee

Bruce Lee Hmm. Emptiness is the Truth. Vacancy is very important. Never think *anything*. Be empty!

Isono You said in the film, *Enter the Dragon*, or *Moeyo Doragon*, "Don't think, feel." Is that the same meaning?

Bruce Lee Ah, don't fear. Don't think about fear! Oh, yeah, it's a great enemy. Fear!

Isono No, no, no, I…

Bruce Lee Fear! Fear is the entity of the devil!

Isono Sorry, my pronunciation was bad.

Bruce Lee Hmm?

Isono I said, "Don't think, *feel*."

ブルース・リー うん。空こそが真理である。空虚こそが極めて重要である。決して何も考えるな。「空」になれ！

磯野 あなたは「燃えよドラゴン」という映画の中で、「考えるな、感じろ」とおっしゃっていました。それと同じ意味でしょうか。

ブルース・リー ああ、恐れるな。恐怖について考えるな！そう、恐怖は大いなる敵だ！

磯野 いえ、そうではなく……。

ブルース・リー 恐怖！ 恐怖が悪魔の正体である。

磯野 すみません、発音が悪かったのですが。

ブルース・リー ん？

磯野 私は、「考えるな、感じろ」と言ったのです。

Bruce Lee Ah! Feel!

Isono Yes, I said "feel."

Bruce Lee You said "feel"?

Isono Yes. Sorry, my pronunciation was bad.

Bruce Lee I see! I heard *fear*… [*Laughs.*]

Jeet Kune Do is "the world's most beautiful and strongest martial art"

Isono Sorry. You said the Truth is empty and emptiness is the Truth.

Bruce Lee Arrrrghhh! [*Stands up and tries to take off jacket, but sits down.*] Oh, [*looks at the mic on left collar*] something bad?

ブルース・リー　ああ、「feel」ね！

磯野　はい、feel と言いました。

ブルース・リー　feel って言ったのか。

磯野　はい、発音が悪くてすみません。

ブルース・リー　わかった！「fear（恐怖）」かと……（笑）。

截拳道は「世界一、美しくて強い武術」

磯野　すみませんでした。「真理とは空であり、空が真理である」とおっしゃいましたが。

ブルース・リー　あああぁぁぁぁ！（立ち上がって上着を脱ぎかけるが、また座る）、ああ（上着の左襟に付けられたマイクを見ながら）何かまずいな。

Wada Yes, there is a microphone.

Bruce Lee [*Fans himself.*] Hot. This is Bangkok, right?

Isono No.

Bruce Lee Bangkok?

Isono & Wada This is Japan.

Bruce Lee Thailand? No?

Isono Not Thailand.

Wada Japan.

Bruce Lee Japan? Really? Hot [*fanning himself using the Blu-ray disc case*]. Hot, hotter, hottest. India or Thailand. OK, OK. Your question is?

和田　はい、マイクがありますから。

ブルース・リー　（手で扇ぎながら）暑い。ここはバンコクかな。

磯野　いえ。

ブルース・リー　バンコク？

磯野・和田　ここは日本です。

ブルース・リー　タイ？　違うの？

磯野　タイではありません。

和田　日本です。

ブルース・リー　日本？　本当？　暑いな。（ブルーレイディスクのケースをうちわにして扇ぎながら）暑い、暑くて、暑すぎる。インドかタイだろう。まあいいわ。で、質問は？

2 Truth, Beauty, and Justice According to Bruce Lee

Wada You were talking about the spirit of Jeet Kune Do. I would like to ask about the origins of your style. I heard it started with street fighting and then you incorporated…

Bruce Lee Good English!

Wada Thank you, Master Okawa has trained me well.

Bruce Lee You are like an American speaking English…

Isono Actually, she is a…

Wada I am American.

Bruce Lee You are American!? You're American like me?

和田　截拳道の精神についてお話しくださっているところでした。あなたのスタイルの原点についてお聞きしたいと思います。確か、最初はストリート・ファイティングから始まり、そこから取り入れたのが……。

ブルース・リー　英語が上手だね！

和田　ありがとうございます。総裁先生にしっかり鍛えていただきましたので。

ブルース・リー　まるでアメリカ人が英語を話してるみたいな……。

磯野　実は彼女は……。

和田　アメリカ人なんです。

ブルース・リー　アメリカ人なの⁉ 私と一緒？

Wada Yes. Yes.

Bruce Lee Oh, OK, OK, OK.

Wada I also lived in San Francisco, so…

Bruce Lee Oh, OK, OK. San Francisco English is good English. Yeah, it's OK.

Wada You incorporated traditional martial arts as well as boxing…

Bruce Lee Oh, good pronunciation!

Wada And fencing…

Bruce Lee Oh, beautiful, beautiful! [*Mimics Wada.*] "Martial arts!" Ohoho. Yeah, good!

Wada And also dancing [*laughs*]. How did you

和田　はい、そうです。

ブルース・リー　ああ、そうか、そうか、そうか。

和田　私もサンフランシスコに住んでいましたので……。

ブルース・リー　ああ、オーケー、オーケー。サンフランシスコ英語はいい英語だよ。うん、いいじゃない。

和田　あなたは伝統的な武術を取り入れたり、ボクシングや……。

ブルース・リー　ああ、発音がいいね！

和田　それからフェンシングや……。

ブルース・リー　美しい美しい。（和田が話す表情を真似ながら）「武術」！　オホホ。ああ、いいなあ！

和田　それからダンスも（笑）。どのようにして、そういっ

incorporate all these different fields into your martial arts and make it your own style?

Bruce Lee Hmm… My father was an actor, this is one thing. And traditional Chinese people, since the 19th century, used to learn kung fu to defend their or our country. We had been intruded by European people. Kung fu means, for example, Japanese *Joi* (meaning "expelling foreigners"). So, at that time, a man of courage must learn kung fu.

I was a disciple of famous Ip Man and I made a

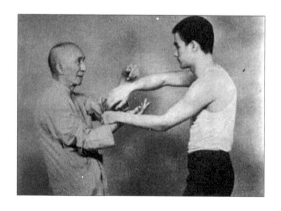

た様々な分野をご自分の武術に取り入れて、独自のスタイルを編み出されたのでしょうか。

ブルース・リー　んー……。父が俳優だったというのが一つと、中国人は19世紀以来、伝統的に、自分たちの国を守るためにカンフーを習うものだったんですよ。中国人はヨーロッパ人の侵略を受けてたから。「カンフー」とは、たとえて言えば、日本語の「攘夷（じょうい）」（外国人を追い払う）という意味なんです。だから当時は、勇気ある男子たる者、カンフーを習わなければならなかったんです。

　私は有名なイップ・マンの弟子になって、盛んにカン

At 14, Bruce Lee (right) learned Wing Chun under Ip Man (left) for approximately four years.
ブルース・リー（右）は14歳のときイップ・マン（左）に弟子入りし、約4年間、詠春拳を学んだ。

lot of propaganda of kung fu. It had been the pride of the Chinese people, especially the Hong Kong people, and including Chinese Americans. I also succeeded in getting a lot of Japanese fans. In the movie world, I overcame karate martial arts or Judo, so kung fu is worldwide through movies.

In this point only, we can make great victory against white people. We must have something great. We must find some greatness in our traditional culture. This was kung fu.

I rebuilt the kung fu tradition and set up a new type of kung fu. It's Jeet Kune Do. It's the world's most beautiful and strongest martial arts, I think. It's also the strongest one and the most beautiful art of human beings. So, here we can find real strength and real beauty, and here we can achieve the Truth.

What is the Truth? It is the criterion which divides good and evil, or God and devils. You know? From the standpoint of justice, we must destroy the bad people.

フーのプロパガンダをやって、それが中国人の、特に香港の人たちや中華系アメリカ人の誇りになったわけです。日本人にも大勢、ファンになってもらえたし。映画の中で私が空手や柔道に勝ったので、カンフーは映画を通して世界的に人気なんです。

　ここだけは、私たちが白人に圧勝できる点なんです。私たちにも、何か優れたところがないといけない。自分たちの伝統文化の中に、何か優秀性を見出さないといけない。それがカンフーだったんですね。

　私はカンフーの伝統を建て直して、新しいタイプのカンフーを始めた。それが「截拳道」です。これこそ、世界一美しく、世界最強の武術だと思ってます。また、最強かつ、人間の芸術の中で最も美しいものでもあります。ここに「本物の強さ」と「本物の美」を見出すことができるし、また、ここにおいて真理にも到達することができるんです。

　真理とは何か。それは善悪を分ける基準であり、神と悪魔を分ける基準です。でしょう？　正義の観点からは、悪しき者たちを倒さねばならない。強くあらねばならな

2 Truth, Beauty, and Justice According to Bruce Lee

You must be strong. You know? You know? You know? Happy Science and Jeet Kune Do are almost the same. [*Slowly turning around on the chair as he shows some Jeet Kune Do moves.*] Woo… Poo. Woo.

On the strength, confidence, and justice of martial artists

Wada You talked about fighting for justice in this world. Would you say that there is a strong relationship between martial arts and religion?

Bruce Lee Religion is the teaching of the heart. How to shape up a pure mind and how to get spirituality in your life. This is religion, the way of religion. It's the same.

Wada I have watched my father practice aikido since I was very young and I always wondered what sort of role the martial artists play in this world. What's their

い。ね？ でしょう？ そうでしょう？ 幸福の科学と截拳道はほとんど同じものですよ。（椅子をゆっくり回転させて截拳道の動きをしながら）ウーーー、プー。ウー。

武術家の「強さ、自信、正義」について

和田　この世における正義のための戦いについて話されました。武術と宗教は密接に関係しているということでしょうか。

ブルース・リー　宗教というのは「心の教え」ですね。人生において、純粋な心を築き上げ、霊性を獲得するための方法です。それが宗教であり、宗教のやり方です。同じです。

和田　私は幼い頃から、父が合気道の稽古をするのを見てきまして、いつも、「武術家には世の中でどういった役割（role）があるんだろう」と思っていました。彼らの使

mission?

Bruce Lee You mean *roll*?

Wada Role. Like the martial artists…

Bruce Lee Oh, San Francisco roll (he may be referring to California roll, a type of sushi)?

Wada Like the mission of a martial artist.

Bruce Lee Mission? Mission. Mission. Mission. OK. Mission. To kill…oh, no. To destroy or knock down evil people. If you're getting stronger and stronger, you can be confident in yourself. At that time, you can be stronger and you can keep justice in your life.

Wada I watched a documentary about you and you were confident to the point where you seemed a little arrogant. Where does your self-confidence come from?

命とは何なのでしょうか。

ブルース・リー　「ロール」って？

和田　役割です。武術家のような人たちは……。

ブルース・リー　ああ、サンフランシスコ・ロール（カリフォルニア巻き〔寿司の一種〕のことと思われる）？

和田　武術家の「使命」のようなものです。

ブルース・リー　使命？　使命ですか。使命ね。わかった、使命ね。悪しき者たちを殺し……じゃなくて粉砕し、倒すことです。強くなればなるほど、自分に自信が持てるようになる。そうすれば、さらに強くなることができ、人生の正義を保つことができるんです。

和田　ブルース・リーさんのドキュメンタリーを見ると、自信満々で、少し傲慢に見えるくらいだったように思います。あなたの自信は、どこから来るのでしょうか。あ

Or, how can we build self-confidence?

Bruce Lee That is the way. The true way is nothing. Nothing is vacancy. Vacancy is emptiness. Emptiness is the Truth. Truth is the world. [*Spreads arms up in the air, turns around while sitting on the chair, and gradually speaks in an excited way.*] World is peace. Peace is universe...

Isono Please calm…

Bruce Lee Universe is, haha, everything! We are in the universe!

るいは、どうすれば自分に自信を持つことができるのでしょうか。

ブルース・リー　そういうものなんですよ。真実の道とは「無」です。「無」とは「空虚」です。「空虚」とは「空」です。「空」とは真理。真理とは世界。（両手を宙に広げて上を見上げ、椅子を回転させて後ろ向きになり、次第に高揚して）世界は平和。平和は宇宙……。

磯野　落ち着いてください……。

ブルース・リー　宇宙は、ハハ、すべて！　われら、宇宙に生きるなり！

3 Taoism and Freedom Believed by Bruce Lee

Asian people can conquer their inferiority complex toward white people by training

Wada I would like to ask you about your career in Hollywood.

Bruce Lee [*Looks at Wada's face.*] Oh, beautiful. Beautiful. Beautiful. Miss beautiful.

Wada [*Laughs.*]

Bruce Lee Beautiful.

Wada OK. You were a Hollywood actor and I think you said in the documentary that it was very difficult to get leading roles in movies because of the discrimination or prejudice against Asian people.

3　ブルース・リーが信じる「タオイズムと自由」

アジア人は鍛錬の力で白人への劣等感に克てる

和田　あなたのハリウッドでの経歴についてお伺いしたいと思います。

ブルース・リー　（和田の顔を見て）ああ、美しいですね。美しい美しい。美人さん。

和田　（笑）

ブルース・リー　お美しい。

和田　はい。あなたはハリウッドの俳優でいらっしゃいましたが、そのドキュメンタリーでは、「アジア人に対する差別や偏見があるので、映画の主役を射止めるのは非常に難しい」とおっしゃっていたと思います。

3 Taoism and Freedom Believed by Bruce Lee

Bruce Lee Asian people. Discrimination against the Asian people.

Wada How did you overcome such discrimination to pursue your career?

Bruce Lee Martial arts or Japanese bushido. These two ways have one purpose, I mean, the Asian people are smaller than the white people. The white people have much pride in their style, I mean they're tall and rich in muscle. They think that pro boxing is the strongest sport in the world and it's a symbol of the white people's strength.

But in Asia, we have kung fu or bushido. Bushido is a different one, so for example, kung fu. If the person who performs kung fu is a small person, or a small man or woman and a slender person, this kind of small, slender person can defeat a great, big, white champion-like boxer or... as you know, Trump, Mr. Trump, the president. The president is big, but if a

84

3　ブルース・リーが信じる「タオイズムと自由」

ブルース・リー　アジア人ね。アジア人への差別ですよ。

和田　ご自分のキャリアを求めるために、どうやってそうした差別を乗り越えていかれたのでしょうか。

ブルース・リー　武術や日本の武士道。この二つの道の目的は一つなんです。要するに、アジア人は白人より小さいでしょう。白人は自分たちのスタイル、要するに背が高いとか筋肉質だとかいうスタイルが、すごく自慢なんですよ。そして、プロ・ボクシングが世界最強のスポーツだと思っていて、それが白人の強さの象徴なんです。

　しかし、アジアにはカンフーがあり武士道がある。武士道は別物なんで、カンフーを例にとりましょう。カンフーをやる人が小柄で、小柄な男性や女性で細身であっても、そういう小柄で細身の人が、巨大な白人のチャンピオンみたいなボクサーや……そう、トランプね。大統領のトランプさんみたいな大きな相手を倒すことができる。トランプ大統領は大きいけど、小柄なアジア人がカ

85

small Asian fights with kung fu, Mr. Trump will be knocked down in 60 seconds, I think, one minute or so. It's the starting point of conquering the inferiority complex of the Asian people, I think.

The starting point is how to control your mind and how to make discipline every day, become a confident man or woman and believe in yourself that we have something stronger or we have something more important in us than the spirit of white people or the muscle of white people. So, we are equal in this meaning. Training conquers everything. Not by nature, but by training we can win and we can conquer everything.

Taoism is the Truth of the world

Isono You are a great martial artist and great philosopher, I think.

Bruce Lee Uh-huh.

ンフーで戦えば、トランプさんも60秒で、たぶん1分か
そこらでノック・ダウンされてしまう。これが、アジア
人が劣等感を克服するための出発点だと思います。

　出発点は、いかに心を統御し、日々、いかに修行を重
ねるかです。そして自信に満ちた男性や女性となり、「自
分たちの中には、白人の精神や白人の筋力より強いもの、
もっと大切なものがあるんだ」と信じることです。その
意味で、われわれは平等なんです。鍛錬は、すべてに克つ。
生まれつきではなく、鍛錬によって勝利し、すべてに打
ち克つことができるのです。

タオイズム（道教）こそ世界の真理

磯野　あなたは偉大な武術家であると同時に、偉大な哲
学者でもあると思います。

ブルース・リー　うん。

3 Taoism and Freedom Believed by Bruce Lee

Isono Because you studied philosophy at university and you studied a wide variety of philosophies from eastern philosophy like Chinese Lao-tzu or Chuang-tzu…

Bruce Lee [*Performing some moves as he listens, and reacts to the name Lao-tzu.*] Lao-tzu, ah, Lao-tzu is good.

Isono …yes, to western philosophy. What kind of philosophy helped you to succeed?

Bruce Lee Taoism is good.

Isono Taoism?

Bruce Lee Yeah, good. Taoism is good. White is black. Black is white. That is the true explanation… that is the Truth of the world. The world's phenomenon is, something is black while something is white. Black and

3　ブルース・リーが信じる「タオイズムと自由」

磯野　あなたは大学で哲学を学び、中国の老子や荘子などの東洋哲学から……。

ブルース・リー　（アクションをしながら質問を聞いているが、老子の名前に反応して）老子、ああ、老子はいいね。

磯野　……はい、西洋哲学にいたるまで、幅広い哲学を学ばれたからです。どのような哲学が、あなたの成功に役立ったのでしょうか。

ブルース・リー　タオイズム（道教）はいいよ。

磯野　タオイズムですか。

ブルース・リー　そう、いいね。タオイズムはいいですよ。白は黒で、黒は白。それこそが真の説明というか……それこそが世界の真理です。世界の事象は、あるものは黒く、あるものは白い。この世界は黒と白で、できている。人は、

white make up this world. We cannot live in the white world only or the black world only. We live through these two colored worlds. You must know.

But choose white. If you look at the black world, but go straight, then after that, you can find the white world. In this meaning, "white" doesn't mean the white people. It just means innocent. I mean innocent. Goodness. "Black" means evil or contaminated. I mean that. People sometimes are contaminated by evil thinking, evil tradition, evil culture, or Hitler-like thinking. But we can be white from black. Black

白い世界にだけ生きることも、黒い世界にだけ生きることもできない。人は、この「二色の世界」の中で生きていることを知らねばならない。

されど、白を選ぶことです。黒い世界が見えていても、まっすぐに進むことです。その先に白い世界が見えてくる。ここで「白」と言っているのは白人のことではなくて、「無垢」という意味にほかなりません。無垢という意味です。「善」のことです。「黒」とは悪、あるいは「汚染されている」という意味です。人は、悪しき考えや悪しき伝統や、悪しき文化や、ヒトラー的な考え方に染まることがあります。しかし、黒から白になれるんです。黒が

The Jeet Kune Do emblem. In the center is the symbol representing the concepts of yin and yang, as in Taoism. The arrows represent the endless interaction between yin and yang and have Bruce Lee's quote, "Using no way as way, having no limitation as limitation."

截拳道のマーク。道教のシンボルである陰陽を表す図を中心に、「それが永遠に回転し、進化する」という意味の矢印があり、「無法をもって有法となし、無限をもって有限となす」というブルース・リーの言葉が配置されている。

3 Taoism and Freedom Believed by Bruce Lee

sometimes turns out to be white.

Taoism is the Truth. It's the Truth. [*While drawing a big imaginary wave with both hands.*] Our life is like the wave, so sometimes we are in the bottom of the wave and sometimes we are in the upmost point of the wave. Devils usually attack us when we are at the top of the wave. Also, devils attack us when we are in the depths of the wave, but at the same time, angels come to save us. So, the top of the wave and the bottom of the wave, these two points have the truth, in this wavelength, as you know.

Can you understand? [*Turns around on the chair, facing back to the interviewers.*] You cannot, of course… [*Stands up with back facing the interviewers, and throws a right kick.*] Acho! [*Turns around and faces the interviewers, then walks toward Sakai.*] Hmm. You're a fighter. You must fight [*takes a fighting stance*].

Sakai [*Laughs.*] No, no, no. Debate, debate.

白だとわかることもある。

タオイズムは真理です。真理なんです。（両手で大きな波の上下を描きながら）私たちの人生は波のようなもので、その底にいるときもあれば、波の頂点にいるときもある。悪魔が攻撃してくるのは、たいていの場合、人が波の頂点にいるときです。波の底にいるときにも悪魔は攻撃してくるけど、そのときは同時に、天使が救いにきてくれる。ですから、「波の頂上」と「波の底」、この二つのポイントの両方に、ご存じの通り、波長の真実があるわけです。

おわかりですか。（椅子を180度回転させて質問者たちに背を向け）わからんでしょう、無理もない……。（後ろを向いたまま立ち上がって右キック）アチョー！　（正面に向き直って酒井の前に進み）ふーむ。君は戦士だろう。戦わなきゃ駄目だ（ファイティングポーズをとる）。

酒井　（笑)いえいえいえ。話し合いましょう。話し合いで。

3 Taoism and Freedom Believed by Bruce Lee

Bruce Lee OK, OK [*sits down on the chair*].

[*Interviewers laugh.*]

"I believe in God"

Sakai Could you tell us, Mr. Bruce Lee, have you ever seen an angel?

Bruce Lee Oh! Yeah, of course.

Sakai Angel?

Bruce Lee [*Points to Wada.*] Angel. Here.

Sakai Other angels?

Bruce Lee [*Points to Sakai.*] Devil.

ブルース・リー　オーケー、オーケー（椅子に座る）。

（質問者　笑）

「私は神を信じている」

酒井　ブルース・リーさんは天使を見たことはあります
か。

ブルース・リー　ああ！ それは、ありますよ。

酒井　天使ですよ？

ブルース・リー　（和田を指差して）天使でしょう？ ここ
にいるから。

酒井　ほかの天使は？

ブルース・リー　（酒井を指差して）悪魔でしょう？

3 Taoism and Freedom Believed by Bruce Lee

[*Audience laugh.*]

Bruce Lee [*Points to Isono.*] Common man.

Sakai What are the criteria to tell between an angel and a devil?

Bruce Lee Your heart is black [*audience laugh*]. [*Points to Wada.*] Her heart is white.

Sakai Yes, I see.

Isono What about me?

Bruce Lee You are mediu...

Wada Medium?

Bruce Lee You are medium… [*laughs*] medium rare.

（一同　笑）

ブルース・リー　（磯野を指差して）普通の人でしょう？

酒井　天使と悪魔を分ける基準は何ですか。

ブルース・リー　君の心は黒いけど（一同　笑）。（和田を指して）彼女の心は白いから。

酒井　はい、わかりました。

磯野　私はどうですか。

ブルース・リー　君は、中……。

和田　中間（ミディアム）ですか。

ブルース・リー　君は中間……（笑）ミディアム・レアだ。

3 Taoism and Freedom Believed by Bruce Lee

Wada Gray color?

Bruce Lee [*Points to Isono.*] Not well-done. He (Sakai) is well-done.

Wada It seems that you are a very spiritual person.

Bruce Lee Uh-huh. Spiritual.

Wada Do you believe in God?

Bruce Lee Oh, of course, of course! I believe in God and I'm God, too. [*Facing Wada.*] You! Of course, you can find gods or goddesses. We are gods or goddesses. Or, sons or daughters of God or Buddha.

Bruce Lee speaks about harmony and energy of the universe

Isono We think that God has many aspects.

98

和田　グレーですか。

ブルース・リー　（磯野を指して）ウェルダンじゃないね。彼（酒井）はウェルダン。

和田　あなたはとても霊的な方のようですね。

ブルース・リー　うん、霊的ですよ。

和田　神を信じていらっしゃいますか。

ブルース・リー　ああ、当然でしょう！　神は信じてるし、私も神ですから。（和田のほうを向いて）君！　君も当然、神や女神に会えますよ。私たちは神であり女神だからね。それか、神仏の息子であり娘だから。

宇宙の調和とエネルギーを語る

磯野　私たちの考えでは、神は様々な側面をお持ちです。

3 Taoism and Freedom Believed by Bruce Lee

Bruce Lee Uh-huh.

Isono Or characteristics. So, what kind of aspects of God do you represent?

Bruce Lee Aspects?

Isono Yes.

Bruce Lee Ah. Hmm... Righteousness.

Isono Righteousness?

Bruce Lee And braveness. Righteousness… braveness… hmm… equality! And freedom! Prosperity! And… love! Peace! Harmony! And receive everything in harmony! Universal harmony! Hmm.

Wada Did you receive any spiritual inspiration?

3　ブルース・リーが信じる「タオイズムと自由」

ブルース・リー　うん。

磯野　あるいは、性質です。あなたは、神のどういった側面を表していらっしゃるのですか。

ブルース・リー　側面？

磯野　はい。

ブルース・リー　ああ。うーん……「正しさ」です。

磯野　正しさですか。

ブルース・リー　それから「勇気」。正しさ……勇気……うーん……「平等」！ そして「自由」！「繁栄」！ そして……「愛」！「平和」！「調和」！ そして、調和の内にすべてを受け取る！「宇宙的調和」！ うん。

和田　何か霊的なインスピレーションを受けていらっしゃいましたか。

101

3 Taoism and Freedom Believed by Bruce Lee

Bruce Lee [*Preoccupied with his moves, he misses the question.*] Hmm?

Wada Did you receive any spiritual inspiration from Heaven?

Bruce Lee Uh–huh.

Wada Do you know who it was from?

Bruce Lee Lao–tzu. Lao–tzu. Lao–tzu.

Isono Lao–tzu? So, Lao–tzu guided you spiritually?

Bruce Lee Taoism is my real spiritual parent. I'm the son of Taoism.

Isono I think you are also influenced by Buddhism.

３　ブルース・リーが信じる「タオイズムと自由」

ブルース・リー　（アクションをしていて聞いていなかった）うん？

和田　天上界から何か霊的なインスピレーションを受けていらっしゃいましたか。

ブルース・リー　うん。

和田　誰からだったか、おわかりですか。

ブルース・リー　老子。老子ですね。老子です。

磯野　老子ですか。では、老子が霊的にあなたを指導していたと。

ブルース・リー　タオイズムが、私の本当の霊的な親ですね。私はタオイズムの申し子です。

磯野　仏教の影響も受けておられると思いますが。

103

3 Taoism and Freedom Believed by Bruce Lee

Bruce Lee Ah, of course, of course. Lao-tzu and Buddha have almost the same direction of thinking. Buddha taught us, "We have the chance to become Buddha because we have Buddha-nature in us. So, we need spiritual training." Sometimes we need some kind of physical training, even in Buddhism.

Taoism is a little different, but Taoism also has training. The training is how you feel the energy of the universe. [*Gesturing with both hands.*] Energy of the universe, you gather that kind of energy from the universe within you, and be relaxed. After that, you concentrate [*stands up*] and attack! [*Throws a punch toward Isono. Isono leans back. Bruce Lee sits back down.*] That is the Truth.

Freedom means to be free from physical bondage

Isono Thank you for your precious lesson. I would

ブルース・リー　ああ、もちろん受けてますよ。老子も仏陀も、思想の方向性は、ほとんど同じですね。仏陀が説かれたのは、「私たちには内なる仏性があるから、仏陀になるチャンスがある。だから霊的修行が必要なのだ」ということですし、仏教でも肉体修行が必要なこともあります。

　タオイズムは少し違うけど、タオイズムにも修行がある。その修行とは、いかに宇宙のエネルギーを「感じるか」です。（両手のジェスチャーで表現しながら）宇宙のエネルギーを、そういうエネルギーを宇宙から自分の内に集めて、そしてリラックスする。そこから精神統一して（立ち上がり）そして、攻撃する！（磯野に向かって突きの動作。磯野、のけぞる。ブルース・リー、椅子に戻る）これが真理です。

自由とは「肉体の束縛からの解放」

磯野　貴重なレッスンをありがとうございます。さらに

3 Taoism and Freedom Believed by Bruce Lee

also like to ask, what is true liberty?

Bruce Lee Liberty?

Isono Yes. Freedom.

Bruce Lee Ah, liberty. Liberty Island.

Isono No, not Liberty Island [*laughs*].

Bruce Lee Liberty. Hmm. Ah, goddess, the Goddess of Liberty (Statue of Liberty). I know, I know.

Isono Yes.

Bruce Lee What's that? What's the problem?

Isono No, no.

Bruce Lee It's… ah, the Goddess of Liberty. Ah, uh-

伺いたいのですが、真の自由（liberty）とは何でしょうか。

ブルース・リー　自由？

磯野　はい、自由（フリーダム）です。

ブルース・リー　ああ、自由(リバティ)ねえ。リバティ島ね。

磯野　いえ、リバティ島ではなくて（笑）。

ブルース・リー　自由か。うーん。ああ、女神、〝自由の女神〟ね。知ってる知ってる。

磯野　はい。

ブルース・リー　それが何？　何が問題なの。

磯野　いえいえ。

ブルース・リー　それは……ああ、自由の女神、ああ、そう。

huh. In that, it's empty. Emptiness. There is emptiness. Yeah, it's true.

Isono So, in your teachings, liberty means empty?

Bruce Lee No, no.

Isono No?

Bruce Lee Freedom first.

Isono Freedom first?

Bruce Lee Freedom. Please set your body free. Set your...ah, your spirit. Please set your spirit free from your bondage, it means your physical condition. This is the true you, yourself.

あの中は空っぽなんですよ。「空」。空がある。その通り。

磯野　では、あなたの教えでは、自由とは「空」であると。

ブルース・リー　いやいや。

磯野　違いますか。

ブルース・リー　まずは「自由（フリーダム）」ですね。

磯野　まず自由ですか。

ブルース・リー　自由です。肉体を自由に解放し……あ、「精神」だ。精神を縛りから解放してください。縛りとは要するに、肉体的条件のことです。それが「真の自己」なのです。

4 China, Japan, and North Korea as Analyzed by Bruce Lee

Bruce Lee spread the Chinese spirit to the world through kung fu

Wada You seem to have a very philosophical side to you. Why did you pursue a career as an actor? You were already a prominent figure in the world of martial arts.

Bruce Lee The Chinese people have a 5,000-year history. They are proud of that history. But since the war between China and Europe, in 1840 or so, we have been destroyed by European pragmatism. It's technology regarding war.

But the Chinese people need some symbol like a flag. For example, the American flag or the flag which was held by the Goddess of Freedom, like that. I'm a flag. I am the flag and I am the symbol. I'm the hero of

4　ブルース・リーが分析する「中国、日本、北朝鮮」

カンフーで世界に中国精神を広めた

和田　あなたは非常に哲学的な面もお持ちのようですが、なぜ俳優の道に進まれたのでしょうか。もうすでに、武術の世界で傑出した人物でいらしたのに。

ブルース・リー　中国人には5000年の歴史があって、その歴史が誇りではあるんだけど、1840年頃のヨーロッパとの戦争以降は、ヨーロッパのプラグマティズム（実用主義）に破壊され続けてきたんです。軍事技術ですね。

　しかし中国人には、何か「旗印」が必要なんです。だからたとえば、アメリカ人にとっての旗、自由の女神が振っている旗のようなものですね。私は「旗」なんです。私が「旗」であり、「旗印」なんです。私は中国人のヒーロー

the Chinese people. Not only the Chinese people, but also the American people, the Japanese people, other Asian people or European people loved me and admired me a lot. It's one kind of patriotism dispatched by me, but the Chinese people need some kind of symbol.

So, I am Paul. Paul-of-Christianity-like existence. I mean, I am Paul of kung fu because I spread the beautiful side and the strong side of kung fu. It's a pride of the Chinese spirit, so I spread this kind of Chinese spirit all over the world.

The Chinese people are one-fifth of the world's population, but for a long time, they have been under, how do I say, "the inferiority complex syndrome." So, I am the destroyer of the inferiority complex of the Chinese. I want to be one of the avengers of the U.S.A. As you know, the U.S.A. has several heroes. I want to be one of the heroes of the Americans.

But it was a little difficult, even for me. My wife was a real American citizen, but we, the Chinese, like the Japanese people, were discriminated by white

4 ブルース・リーが分析する「中国、日本、北朝鮮」

です。中国人だけでなく、アメリカ人や日本人や、その他のアジア人やヨーロッパ人も、私をすごく愛して崇めてくれました。 それは私から発信された一種の愛国心が理由なんですが、中国人には何かシンボルが必要なんです。

ですから、私は〝パウロ〟なんです。キリスト教のパウロみたいな存在なんです。つまり、「カンフーのパウロ」ですね。カンフーの美しさや強さを広めたので。それが中国精神の誇りだから、私はそういった中国精神を世界中に広めたんです。

中国人は世界の人口の五分の一を占めているのに、長い間、何というか、「劣等感症候群」に陥っていたんで、私は中国人の劣等感の破壊者であって、アメリカの「アベンジャーズ」の一人になりたいんです。ご存じの通り、アメリカにはヒーローが何人かいますが、私はアメリカ人のヒーローの一人になりたいと思ってます。

でも、いくら私でも、それはやや難しいことであって、妻は純粋なアメリカ人でしたが、われわれ中国人は日本人同様、白人アメリカ人から差別されていたんです。私

113

Americans. I sometimes said, "American people say that men are equal and we have freedom and liberty. They say so. But it means equality belongs to white people and freedom and liberty also belong to white people." They despised and disregarded black people and yellow people. When I got married and had a baby, my mother-in-law said, "Oh, I'm going to have a yellow baby." She said so. I was very sorry. I was born in America, but I was physically from China. They had discrimination then.

So, I am the representative of the colored people. Chinese people sometimes dislike the Japanese or sometimes dislike the Korean people, but we must be friends on this point. We must say, "Our soul is equal to the white people." I mean, white, black, and yellow are the same—they all come from God or Buddha.

So, we must show something against the superiority of the white people. In my case, this was kung fu and it got the Hollywood movies involved. It's a very popular way and an effective way for the world. What

はこう言ったこともありましたよ。「アメリカ人は、『人間は平等で、自由がある』と言うくせに、要は、その『平等』とは白人のものであり、『自由』も白人のものなんだ」と。黒人や黄色人種は軽蔑され、無視されていました。私が結婚して子供が生まれるとき、妻の母が言った言葉は、「ああ、黄色の赤ん坊が生まれるのね」と、そう言ったんですよ。すごく悲しかったですね。私はアメリカで生まれたけど、肉体的には中国人ですから。当時は差別がありました。

　だから、私は有色人種の代表なんです。中国人は、日本人を嫌ったり韓国人を嫌ったりすることもありますが、この点に関しては仲良くしないといけません。「われわれの魂は白人と平等なんだ」と言わなければいけません。白人も黒人も黄色人種も同じなんです。皆、神仏から生まれてきたんです。

　だから、白人優越主義に対して、何かを示さないといけない。私の場合は、それがカンフーであり、ハリウッド映画を巻き込んでいったわけです。映画は世界的に、非常に人気があって効果的な方法ですからね。真の中国

is the real Chinese spirit and what is the strength of the Chinese people? This was my mission.

[*Speaks to Isono in a joking manner.*] You asked if I'm in Heaven. It's Japanese discrimination against the Chinese. Please apologize to the Chinese people.

Isono No, I don't mean any evil intention toward you.

Bruce Lee Really?

Bruce Lee's name engraved in the Hollywood Walk of Fame. Located on Hollywood Boulevard. Having a name engraved on the Walk of Fame is the greatest honor in Hollywood.
ブルース・リーの名が刻まれた「ハリウッド・ウォーク・オブ・フェーム」。ハリウッド大通りに設置されている。ここに名を連ねることは、ハリウッド最高の栄誉とされる。

4 ブルース・リーが分析する「中国、日本、北朝鮮」

精神とは何であり、中国人の強さとは何なのか。それが私の使命でした。

（冗談めいた表情で、磯野に向けて）君は、私が天国にいるかと聞いてきたけど、それは日本人の中国人に対する差別ですよ。中国人に謝ってください。

磯野 いえ、悪意はまったくありませんので。

ブルース・リー　本当ですか。

A bronze statue stands in Los Angeles, where Bruce Lee once lived.
ブルース・リーが一時期住んでいたロサンゼルスには、彼の銅像が立っている。

Isono Yes.

Wada It's a question we ask many spirits regardless of their race.

Bruce Lee Uh-huh.

Movies are a new weapon

Isono You succeeded in spreading the spirit of kung fu all over the world through your movies.

Bruce Lee Uh-huh.

Isono So, I'd like to ask about the mission of movies. What do you think is the mission of movies today?

Bruce Lee They are a new weapon for the people. I mean, if we want to know something through

4　ブルース・リーが分析する「中国、日本、北朝鮮」

磯野　はい。

和田　人種にかかわりなく、多くの霊人にお聞きする質問なんです。

ブルース・リー　ああ、そうなの。

映画は「新たな武器」である

磯野　あなたは映画を通して、世界中にカンフーの精神を広めることに成功されました。

ブルース・リー　うん。

磯野　そこで、映画の使命についてお伺いしたいのですが、現代における「映画の使命」とは何であると思われますか。

ブルース・リー　映画は人々にとっての「新たな武器」ですよ。新聞で何かを知ろうと思ったら読み書きを習わ

newspapers, we must learn how to read or write, or do difficult studying, but when we just watch TV or movies, we can be relaxed and understand or accept something great. It's an easy way and a popular way; spreading of the Truth by movie has ten times the power or one hundred times the power if we compare it to writing a book or something like that, so it's very convenient.

You too, use movies more and more. It's very convenient, and it's easy to be a hero through movies. But the reading population cannot be so many, so it's very difficult.

The Communist Party of China will collapse within 10 years

Wada You talked about equality amongst races, but there are many kung fu movies with strong anti-Japanese sentiment.

ないといけないし、難しい勉強もしないといけない。でも、テレビや映画を見るだけなら、リラックスしながら、大きなテーマのことも理解して受け入れることができるわけです。簡単で大衆受けする手段なので、映画で真理を広めるのは本を書いたりするのと比べて10倍、100倍のパワーがあって、すごく便利なんです。

あなたたちも、もっともっと映画を使ってください。すごく便利で、映画を通してヒーローになるのは簡単ですよ。読書人口は、そんなに増やせないから、非常に難しいですね。

中国共産党は10年以内に崩壊する

和田　人種間における平等についてお話しくださいましたが、強い反日感情が描かれているカンフー映画もたくさんあります。

Bruce Lee Anti-Japanese, OK.

Wada Also, in China, there is a strong trend to hate Japanese people. What do you think about that?

Bruce Lee In my days, China's economic power was very small. Japan was the rising sun at that time, in my days in the 1960s or 70s. At that time, Japan was the sun in the sky and we were just in the light of the moon.

But nowadays, 40 years have passed since then. The Chinese people are getting greater in the economy and have military power now. But they are on the way. I think so. It is said that the Chinese economy is larger than the Japanese one, but in Japan, there are 10 million… no, no, 100 million people. We have more than… I don't know correctly, but ten times as many people as Japan. So, even if the economic size of China is larger than the Japanese one, it does not mean that Japan is inferior to China. Japan has an industrious

4　ブルース・リーが分析する「中国、日本、北朝鮮」

ブルース・リー　反日ね、なるほど。

和田　また、中国には、日本人を嫌う傾向が強くあります。それについては、どのようにお考えですか。

ブルース・リー　私の頃は、中国の経済力はすごく小さくて、私が生きてた1960年代、70年代当時は、日本が日の出の勢いでしたからね。あの頃は、日本と言えば、もう、空にかかる太陽で、私たちのほうは月の光に照らされているようなものでした。

　でも今は、あれから40年経って、中国人の経済力が大きくなってるし、今は軍事力もある。ただ、彼らはまだ途中段階だと思いますよ。中国の経済は日本より大きいと言ったって、日本の人口は1千万……、いやいや、1億で、われわれの人口は……正確には知りませんけど、日本の10倍以上ありますからね。だから、中国の経済規模が日本より大きいとしても、日本が中国より劣っているわけじゃない。日本には勤勉な心、勤勉の精神があって、日本はこの150年間、アジアの人々にとっての憧れの的なんです。

123

mind or spirit, and Japan has been the icon of the Asian people for the last 150 years.

Now, the Chinese people think that we can catch up to Japan and overcome Japan this time. They think so, but I think it's a little difficult. Japan is the first country of the Asian countries which defeated European countries, so we must learn something more from Japan. I think so.

China, Korea and Japan, these three must be friends. We must keep the friendship and protect the Asian area from the intrusion of Anglo-Saxon people. China has been intruded many, many times and only Japan could show that power. We must learn from each other and make a tie between us. It's very important, I think. We are not enemies. We must be friends. I think so.

Sakai About China, what do you think about the Communist Party of China and Xi Jinping administration? What do you think about it now?

4 ブルース・リーが分析する「中国、日本、北朝鮮」

　中国人は今、「今度こそ日本に追いつき追い越せる」と思ってるけど、それはちょっと難しいでしょうね。日本は、アジアで初めてヨーロッパ諸国を打ち負かした国なので、私たちはもっと日本に学ばないといけないと思いますよ。

　中国、韓国、日本、この三つは友人にならないといけません。友好関係を保ち、アングロサクソンの侵略からアジア地域を守らなければいけません。かつての中国は何度も何度も侵略されて、日本だけが、そういう力を示すことができたんです。互いに学び合って、絆を結ばないといけません。それが非常に大事なことであると思います。私たちは敵同士ではありません。友人でなければいけないと思います。

酒井　中国に関してですが、中国共産党と習近平政権についてはどう思われますか。現時点で、どう思われますか。

125

Bruce Lee About the communist party, I think China is changing greatly now. I feel a great wave from Hong Kong and the south part of China. China is a country of capitalism now in reality, but they have an illusion that they belong to communism. It's not true. They are living in capitalism.

Japan is now going from capitalism to socialism. I think so. Japan is just seeking equality, not the growth of the economy, but equality in the result of economic activity.

But look at China. They are seeking wealth and they are working for their own wealth ardently. Quite different. China is just in the Meiji period of Japan. Changing, changing, changing, changing.

So, the Communist Party of China will collapse in the near future, I mean within 10 years because the Chinese economic size is a very huge one. It's competing with the American economy. It means China will change into a capitalist country, for the Chinese people

４　ブルース・リーが分析する「中国、日本、北朝鮮」

ブルース・リー　共産党に関しては、中国は今、大きく変わろうとしていると思いますね。香港や中国南部から〝大きな波〟が押し寄せているのを感じます。今の中国は、現実には資本主義の国になってるのに、「共産主義陣営に属している」という幻想を抱いていますが、それは真実じゃない。彼らは資本主義の中に生きてるんです。

　今は日本のほうが、資本主義から社会主義に進んでいると思います。日本は平等性ばかり求めて、経済成長は求めてない。求めているのは経済活動の結果平等です。

　しかし、中国を見てくださいよ。豊かさを求めて、自分が豊かになりたいと思って一生懸命働いてるでしょう。まったく違うんです。中国はちょうど、日本の明治時代をやってるところなんです。変わるところですね、変わるところなんです。

　ですから近い将来、10年以内に、中国共産党は崩壊するでしょう。中国の経済規模は非常に大きくなって、アメリカ経済と競争してますからね。これは、中国が資本主義国に変わるということです。中国国民は金儲けのために生きてるからです。ご存じの通り、彼らは精神面の

127

are living to earn money. As you know, they don't have much intention in spiritual development, but I think, as you know, people need food and livelihood, I mean food, house and clothes. After that, people can seek a pure spiritual living.

China is just moving, so don't think too rapidly about that. They will become a Japanese-like country and an American-like country in these 10 or 20 years. And, the beginning of capitalism, I mean the culture which allows you to get money from huge reputation, started from Bruce Lee. I'm the starting point of capitalism of the Hong Kong Chinese [*laughs*].

Isono OK. Then, I'd like to ask about the current situation in China and Hong Kong, since we are greatly concerned about that. The Chinese government suppresses the liberty of the Chinese people and there is the "one country, two systems" policy in Hong Kong, but the Chinese government invaded and deprived the people of Hong Kong of their liberty. So, what do you

向上に関しては大した意図を持っていないんですが、私が思うに、人間には衣食住が必要であって、それがそろって初めて、純粋な精神生活を求めることができるようになるんです。

　中国は今まさに変化している最中なので、あまり性急に考えないようにしてください。今後10年、20年で、日本やアメリカのような国に変わっていくでしょう。そして、資本主義の始まりは、要するに、大きな名声を得てお金を稼ぐことを許容する文化の始まりは、ブルース・リーだった。私が、香港中国人の〝資本主義の始まり〟なんです（笑）。

磯野　はい。では、中国と香港の現状について伺いたいと思います。私たちはこの点を非常に懸念（けねん）しています。中国政府は中国人民の自由を抑圧しています。また、香港では「一国二制度」が採（と）られていますが、中国政府は香港市民の自由を侵し、奪っています。この現状について、どうお考えでしょうか。

think about the current situation?

Bruce Lee Then, how about Duterte of the Philippines? He killed a lot because of his policy on drugs.

Isono Hmm.

Bruce Lee More than China. He killed a lot of people. Maybe seven hundred or eight hundred thousand? I'm not sure, but maybe almost one million people were killed by President Duterte because of drug dealers or drug users*. It's more than the Chinese government, I think. America usually attacks Chinese policies because of the lack of humanity. It means the government puts pressure on weaker people or poor people. But now, even America cannot say like that because America itself has very much difference between the richest

---

* In reality, it is reported that several thousand people were killed during his search for drug users, and a million turned themselves in out of fear of being killed.

ブルース・リー じゃあ、フィリピンのドゥテルテはどうなんですか。麻薬を理由に大勢、殺したけど。

磯野 うーん。

ブルース・リー 中国以上ですよ。国民を大勢殺したでしょう。70万か80万……かな？ よく知らないけど、100万近いかもしれない人数が、麻薬売買や麻薬の使用でドゥテルテ大統領に殺された（注）。これは中国政府以上だと思いますよ。アメリカはいつも中国の政策を、人道に反すると言って攻撃してきます。中国政府が弱者や貧しい人を抑圧しているという意味ですが、今はアメリカでも最富裕層と最貧困層の格差が大きく開いてるんで、そんなことが言えた義理じゃない。アメリカも中国と同じようなもんですよ。

（注）実際は、麻薬捜査の過程で殺された人は千人単位の人数で、殺害を恐れて出頭した人が100万人と言われている。

people and the poorest people. So, America is almost the same as China.

We must think about that seriously, of course. But firstly, there are the people who are talented in something, for example, kung fu, being beautiful, writing books, teaching something or showing something, and getting great money. After that, people learn from them and follow them. And after that, social welfare must remake the country politics. I think so.

As you said, China has a lot of problems, but 30 or 40 years ago, I mean in my age, in my period, almost all Chinese people were very poor at that time. But now, 20 or 30 percent of the Chinese people are richer than before. It's getting better and better, so just give them the time.

And, a lot of Chinese people have been going abroad, especially to the United States, studying in the United States universities or getting an MBA from a famous university in the U.S.A., and returning back to China. Now, they are still not so old; they are 20,

4 ブルース・リーが分析する「中国、日本、北朝鮮」

　もちろん、それについては真剣に考えないといけませんが、まずは、何か才能がある人、たとえばカンフーとか、美人であるとか、本を書けるとか、何かを教えたり見せたりできるとか、大金を稼げるとか、そういう人たちがいて、その次に、みんながその人に学んで、ついていくようになる。社会福祉によって国内政治を作り直さないといけないのは、その後の話だと思います。

　おっしゃる通り、中国にはいろいろ問題がありますが、30 年、40 年前の私の時代には、中国人はほとんど全部、非常に貧しい人ばかりでした。でも今は、20 から 30 パーセントの中国人は前より豊かになっている。だんだんよくなってはいるので、時間を与えてやってください。

　そして、中国人の多くが海外に出て、特にアメリカに行って、アメリカの大学で学んだり、アメリカの有名大学でＭＢＡを取ったりして、中国に帰ってきてます。彼らはまだ、そんなに歳もいってなくて、20 歳、30 歳、40 歳ぐらいだけど、この先 10 年、20 年もすれば、政治面や

133

4 China, Japan, and North Korea as Analyzed by Bruce Lee

30, or 40 years old. But 10 or 20 years in the future, they will get real influence on politics, economy, and education. Then, China will change greatly. I hope so.

Isono Does that mean you support the current Chinese government's policies?

Bruce Lee No. I don't support. I just said I'm the first one.

There will be another hero after Liu Xiaobo

Isono So next, the future generations of China will change the government or regime?

Bruce Lee The Chinese people need a hero, and I am the hero. One part of Chinese culture is kung fu, but there are other parts of the culture. Other heroes will appear after me and follow me. They will continue to fight against all systems and they will finally win. I

134

経済面や教育面で実際に影響力を持つようになるでしょう。それによって中国が大きく変わっていってほしいというのが、私の願いです。

磯野　では、あなたは現在の中国政府の政策を支持しているということでしょうか。

ブルース・リー　いや。支持はしてません。「私が最初だ」と言っただけです。

劉暁波のあとに「次なるヒーロー」が出る

磯野　では次の質問ですが、中国の将来世代は中国政府、政体を変革するでしょうか。

ブルース・リー　中国人には「ヒーロー」が必要で、私がその「ヒーロー」なんです。中国文化の一部はカンフーですが、それ以外の部分もあります。私のあとに「次なるヒーロー」が出て来て、私に続くでしょうね。彼らがあらゆる制度に対して戦いを続けて、最終的には勝つこ

think so.

Sakai Do you know who Liu Xiaobo is?

Bruce Lee I know.

Sakai He is a hero, I think.

Bruce Lee Uh-huh.

Sakai What do you think about him?

Bruce Lee He's OK, but he is not Bruce Lee. He is before Bruce Lee. After his death, there will appear a Bruce Lee, a political performer, and the political reformer will succeed in the real revolution for freedom. I think so.

China selected economy first and politics later. It was made in the 1980s or 1990s, around then. So, economy first and politics will follow, I think. Xi

とになると思いますよ。

酒井　劉暁波をご存じですか。

ブルース・リー　知ってますよ。

酒井　彼はヒーローだと思うのですが。

ブルース・リー　はい。

酒井　どう思われますか。

ブルース・リー　いいと思うけど、彼は〝ブルース・リー〟ではないですね。〝ブルース・リーの露払い〟であって、彼の死後に〝ブルース・リー〟が出て来て、政治変革者として自由のための真の革命に成功するだろうと思います。

　中国は「経済」を優先して、「政治」を後回しにしたんですよ。1980年代か90年代頃にやったことです。ですから「経済が先で、政治はあとからついてくる」と思います。

Jinping is not so good at developing the economy, so he is just attacking the politicians who get a lot of money by dint of their political power. He says, "We'll kill tigers and flies, both.*" It means a man who has great power and a man who has small power, both who commit crimes will be banished from the Chinese central political position. He insists so. It's an old style. I know it's an old style. It's maybe a style used before the Meiji Restoration, I mean the Edo period, I think. But China is, at this time, at that level, but after that, they will change. I think so.

North Korea should ask Japan to rescue them

Wada I would like to ask about North Korea.

Bruce Lee North Korea!? Ah…

---

* A slogan used by Xi Jinping in his anti-corruption campaign. "Tigers" means high-ranking officials while "flies" means petty civil servants. Simply put, corruptions will be exposed regardless of position.

習近平は経済を発展させるのはあまり得意でないので、政治権力に任せて金儲けをする政治家を締め上げているだけです。彼が「虎もハエも叩く」（注）と言ってるのは、犯罪を働いた人間は、権力が大きかろうが小さかろうが、どちらも政権の中枢から追放するということです。彼はそう言い切ってますが、旧いやり方ですよ。旧いやり方なのはわかってる。明治維新以前の、江戸時代のやり方でしょうね。でも、現時点の中国はそういうレベルなんであって、あとになれば変わっていくと思います。

北朝鮮は日本に救いを求めよ

和田　北朝鮮についてお尋ねしたいと思います。

ブルース・リー　北朝鮮!?　ああ……。

（注）腐敗撲滅キャンペーンのためのスローガン。虎は「幹部クラスの高級官僚」、ハエは「末端の下級官僚」を指す。要するに、「地位を問わず、汚職を摘発する」ということ。

Wada Now, Mr. Trump has been threatening North Korea and the relationship between the United States, China and Japan is very unstable. How can we resolve this or what do you think about this situation?

Bruce Lee Hmm, very complicated because the emotion of North Korean people and South Korean people is very confusing, I mean they are educated to hate Japanese people historically. But they are also taught, "America is the new intruder, so be careful."

Especially, North Korea has no friends. The only friend is China, but China is greatly changing now. China's trading amount is... the China-American trade amount is number one. So, in thinking from the standpoint of trading profit, even Xi Jinping will finally give up on North Korea.

They will choose America because America, the United States, will make China a wealthier country, but North Korea just says, "Give us money. Give us goods. Give us food." It's pity indeed, but as one of the

4　ブルース・リーが分析する「中国、日本、北朝鮮」

和田　現在、トランプ氏が北朝鮮を威嚇しており、アメリカ、中国、日本の関係は非常に不安定になっています。この事態はどうすれば解決できますでしょうか。あるいは、この状況についてどのようにお考えでしょうか。

ブルース・リー　うーん、実に複雑ですね。北朝鮮や韓国の国民感情は、非常に混乱しているというか、歴史的に日本人を憎むように教育されているので。まあ、「アメリカは新たな侵略者だから気をつけろ」とも教わってますけどね。

　特に北朝鮮には、味方がいません。唯一の味方は中国だけど、その中国も今、大きく変わりつつあって、中国の貿易額は……米中の貿易額は一位ですから、貿易上の利益の点から考えれば、習近平も最終的には北朝鮮を見限ることになるでしょうね。

　中国はアメリカを選ぶでしょう。アメリカは中国をもっと豊かにしてくれるけど、北朝鮮はただただ「金をくれ。モノをくれ。食料をくれ」と言うだけなので。実際、気の毒ではあるけれども、世界最大国の一つとして、中国

largest countries of the world, the Chinese top leader, even if it's Xi Jinping or another person, will choose what is big and what is small. They can understand the reason why.

So, North Korea should change their attitude. They don't believe that they will be abandoned by Beijing in the near future, but in reality, Beijing will give up North Korea because they are bad in their behavior.

Also, they are educated to look down upon Japan. But Japan is a strong country and a very intelligent country. All over, the Japanese people can read and learn a lot of knowledge. People who can read, speak, and hear Japanese language… The Japanese language guarantees the people to become intelligent as the world's top level.

Even the Chinese people and the Korean people are proud that they are good at speaking English. They are proud of that, but the Japanese people learn from Japanese books, Japanese news, or Japanese wisdom, how to live and what their future is. The Japanese

の主席は、習近平であっても別の人であっても、物事の大小を選択するでしょう。そうすべきである理由がわかるでしょう。

　ですから、北朝鮮は態度を改めるべきです。もうじき自分たちが中国政府から見捨てられるとは思ってないだろうけど、実際には、北朝鮮の素行が悪いので、中国政府は見捨てるでしょうね。

　それと、彼らは日本を見下すように教育されているけど、日本は強国だし、極めて知的レベルの高い国ですよ。日本人は誰でも字が読めて、多くの知識を学ぶことができる。日本語が読めて話せて聞ける人は……日本国民は日本語のおかげで、世界のトップレベルの知性を保証されてるんです。

　中国人も韓国人も、自分たちは英語が堪能だと自慢してるけど、日本人は、日本語の本やニュースや日本の知恵から、生き方や、自分たちの未来について学んでいるんです。日本人は、ヨーロッパ人や他のアジア人とは正反対です。日本は「もう一つの文明」だと思いますよ。

people are quite contrary to the European people and other Asian people. Japan is another civilization, I think. This is very strong and a very excellent one.

So, North Korea will lose two points. I mean, first, the support of Beijing. And, they must learn from Japan a lot, but they dislike it and they will lose the chance to save themselves. Japan can save North Korea, of course, but their behavior is very bad. So, Japan doesn't work.

The last question is, when will the United States attack North Korea, or will they not attack? Japan is just observer-like people, but North Korea must ask for some rescue from Japan. I think so.

Isono Thank you.

4　ブルース・リーが分析する「中国、日本、北朝鮮」

非常に力のある、優れた文明です。

　だから、北朝鮮は二つ失点を重ねるでしょう。一つは
「中国政府の支援」。そして、（もう一つは）「日本から多
くを学ぶべきなのに、それを嫌がって、自分で自分を救
うチャンスを逃す」ということ。日本は北朝鮮を救うこ
とは、もちろん可能ですが、彼らのやっていることがひ
どすぎるので、日本は動きませんね。

　残された問題は、「いつアメリカが北朝鮮を攻撃するか、
しないか」です。日本人は傍観していますが、北朝鮮は日
本に何らかの救いを求めなければいけないと思いますよ。

磯野　ありがとうございます。

5 Bruce Lee Reveals His Past Life, the Truth of His Death, and the Mission of His Soul

"I was a dragon in every time"

Sakai Another question. I would like to know about your past life. Do you know what your past life is?

Bruce Lee Past life, hmm… [*Picks up and looks at the* Enter the Dragon *Blu-ray disc case*] Dragon [*smiles toward the camera as he shows the case*].

Sakai Dragon? Not human, but a dragon?

Bruce Lee Dragon.

Sakai You are a dragon?

5　ブルース・リーが明かす「過去世、死の真相、魂の使命」

私はいつの時代も「ドラゴン」だった

酒井　もう一つ質問させていただきます。あなたの過去世を知りたいのですが、ご自分の過去世が何であるか、ご存じですか。

ブルース・リー　過去世、うーん……（「燃えよドラゴン」のブルーレイディスクを手に取って眺めながら）「ドラゴン」です（ジャケットをカメラに向けて見せ、ニヤリと<ruby>微笑<rt>ほほえ</rt></ruby>む）。

酒井　ドラゴンですか。人間ではなく、ドラゴンですか。

ブルース・リー　「ドラゴン」です。

酒井　あなたはドラゴンなんですか。

147

Bruce Lee Dragon. A dragon [*laughs*].

Isono Do you mean in this world or in another world?

Bruce Lee Huh? In every time… I was a dragon, I mean a hero.

Isono Have you always been a hero?

Bruce Lee Yeah.

Isono Do you have any memory living in China or other countries?

Bruce Lee Hmm… There have been a lot of dragons in China, Japan, and other Asian countries and of course, in the ancient time, in the Middle East, Africa, and Europe. I have been a dragon.

Sometimes a warrior, of course, of course.

5　ブルース・リーが明かす「過去世、死の真相、魂の使命」

ブルース・リー　ドラゴンです。ドラゴン（笑）。

磯野　この世でという意味ですか、それともあの世でという意味でしょうか。

ブルース・リー　うん？　いつの時代も……「ドラゴン」ですよ。つまり、「ヒーロー」です。

磯野　いつの時代もヒーローでいらしたと。

ブルース・リー　そうです。

磯野　中国や、ほかの国に生きていらした記憶はありますか。

ブルース・リー　うーん……。中国や日本や他のアジアの国には、ドラゴンがたくさんいたんでね。もちろん古代には、中東やアフリカやヨーロッパにもいたし。私はずっと「ドラゴン」です。
　もちろん、「戦士」だったときもありますよ。あるとき

149

Sometimes I was a warrior. And sometimes… [*Thinks for a moment.*] Umm… warrior [*laughs*]. Oh, yeah [*laughs*].

Isono So, you are always a warrior and fighting against evil.

Bruce Lee Yeah.

Sakai What about in Japan?

Bruce Lee Ah, hmm… Maybe a ninja, like that [*laughs*]. *Iga* ninja, like that [*laughs*].

Sakai I heard you were a shogun in the Muromachi *bakufu*.

Bruce Lee Ah, shogun?

Sakai Shogun.

は戦士。またあるときは……（考えて）うん……戦士（笑）。ああ、そういうことです（笑）。

磯野　つまり、いつも戦士であり、悪と戦っていらしたと。

ブルース・リー　そうです。

酒井　日本では？

ブルース・リー　ああ、うーん……。忍者か何かですかね（笑）。伊賀の忍者とか（笑）。

酒井　室町幕府で将軍だったと伺ったのですが。

ブルース・リー　ああ、ショウグンのことですか。

酒井　そうです。

5 Bruce Lee Reveals His Past Life, the Truth of His Death, and the Mission of His Soul

Bruce Lee You say that, but I've heard that in your book, you wrote that Lee Teng-hui of Taiwan was a shogun of Ashikaga bakufu.* So, I must stop my saying. Warrior, just a warrior. It's an easy way, but it's OK.

Sakai But who do you think is the reincarnation of Ashikaga Yoshiteru?

Bruce Lee I don't know, I don't know, I don't know. I was usually a warrior. Maybe I was strong, as strong as Ashikaga Yoshiteru's teacher.

Sakai Tsukahara Bokuden[†]?

---

[*] In his spiritual interview, the guardian spirit of Lee Teng-hui said that he was Yoshiteru Ashikaga, the 13th Shogun of the Muromachi government of Japan, in his past life. See *Japan! Regain Your Samurai Spirit: A Message from the Guardian Spirit of Lee Teng-hui, Former President of the Republic of China* (New York: IRH Press, 2014).

[†] A master swordsman in the late Muromachi period (16th century) of Japan. He is believed to have been the instructor of sword fighting for Yoshiteru Ashikaga.

5　ブルース・リーが明かす「過去世、死の真相、魂の使命」

ブルース・リー　そうは言うけど、あなたがたの本では台湾の李登輝が足利幕府の将軍だと書いてるんでしょう（注1）。それなら、私からは言わないようにしないと。「戦士」です。ただの戦士。安易かもしれませんけど、それで結構ですよ。

酒井　しかし、あなたとしては、誰が足利義輝の転生だと思っているんですか。

ブルース・リー　知りません、知りません、知りません。私は、たいていは戦士だったので。強さの点では、足利義輝の師匠と同じぐらいだったかもしれないけど。

酒井　塚原卜伝（注2）ですか。

（注1）李登輝守護霊は霊言の中で、自らの過去世は室町幕府第13代将軍・足利義輝であると語っている。『日本よ、国家たれ！ 元台湾総統 李登輝守護霊 魂のメッセージ』（大川隆法著・幸福の科学出版刊）参照。

（注2）室町時代後期の剣豪。足利義輝の剣の師匠と言われている。

153

5 Bruce Lee Reveals His Past Life, the Truth of His Death, and the Mission of His Soul

Bruce Lee Tsukahara Bokuden, ah... I don't know exactly, but I must have been some kind of grand master. You have a lot of grand masters in bushido, so please choose a suitable one.

Sakai Suitable one, OK.

Isono I also heard you had a memory of being born as Lin Chong*.

Bruce Lee Oh, it's a fiction.

Isono Fiction?

Bruce Lee It's fiction writing, so...

Isono So, it was not true?

---

* A fictional character in *Water Margin*, a Chinese novel printed in the Ming dynasty in the 16th century. An expert spearman.

154

5　ブルース・リーが明かす「過去世、死の真相、魂の使命」

ブルース・リー　塚原卜伝、ああ……よく知りませんが、何らかのグランド・マスター（師範、剣豪）だったはずです。武士道にはグランド・マスターが大勢いますから、適当な人を選んでください。

酒井　適当な人ですね、はい。

磯野　あなたは林冲（注）として生まれた記憶があるとも伺ったのですが。

ブルース・リー　ああ、それはフィクションですから。

磯野　フィクションですか。

ブルース・リー　作り話ですから……。

磯野　では、真実ではないと。

（注）16世紀（明代）に確立したと言われる中国の小説『水滸伝』に登場する架空の人物。槍の名手。

5 Bruce Lee Reveals His Past Life, the Truth of His Death, and the Mission of His Soul

Bruce Lee But in some meaning, it's true. I'm good at using a spear, you know? Long, sword–like spear. [*Acts as if using a spear.*] Shakespeare*, you know? Yeah. [*Speaks to Sakai.*] As you did (in your past life). You are a master.

Sakai No, no.

Bruce Lee You are a master of spears.

The spiritual truth of his early death

Wada I think you had a very big mission here on earth, but you died very young. Were you able to accomplish everything you were supposed to?

Bruce Lee No.

---

* The name Shakespeare comes from "shake" and "spear."

ブルース・リー　まあ、ある意味では真実ですよ。私は「槍の使い手」なので。だから、長くて剣みたいな槍ですよ。（槍を振る真似）「シェークスピア」（注）ね。わかります？

　そう。（酒井に向かって）あなた（の過去世）と同じで。あなたは名人ですから。

酒井　いえいえ。

ブルース・リー　槍の名人でしょう。

「早すぎた死」のスピリチュアルな真相

和田　あなたは、この地上で非常に大きな使命がおありだったようですが、非常に若くして亡くなられました。やろうと思っていたことを、すべて成し遂げることはできたのでしょうか。

ブルース・リー　いや。

（注）イギリスの劇作家シェークスピア（Shakespeare）の名前は、「槍（spear）を振る（shake）」に由来している。

5 Bruce Lee Reveals His Past Life, the Truth of His Death, and the Mission of His Soul

Wada How did you die?

Bruce Lee [*Sighs deeply.*] I had an accident in my back in my twenties and I did too much in my movies, so it must have been the direct reason of my young death.

Another reason is, I had enemies which could not be seen through my human eyes. I sometimes said devils. Devils were attacking me. Devils don't like heroes. A hero is sometimes the assistant of God, so heroes are targeted by devils. It's like Ryoma Sakamoto, who died too young. He died too young, the same age as when I died. We are on the verge of losing our lives, every year, every age, and every period.

We have a mind of *fushaku shimmyo*,* of course, because we are the destroyers of the old age. So, the people who protect the old age sometimes kill us and even the devils will give powers to them. I was a hero from Heaven, but some devils want to destroy the

---

* A Buddhist term meaning, "devoting one's life."

5　ブルース・リーが明かす「過去世、死の真相、魂の使命」

和田　どのような亡くなり方だったのでしょうか。

ブルース・リー　（大きなため息）20代で腰を痛めて、映画でもやりすぎたので、早死にした直接的原因はそれでしょうね。

　もう一つには、人間の眼には見えない敵がいたんですよ。「悪魔」と言ったこともありましたが、悪魔に攻撃されてたんです。悪魔はヒーローが好きじゃないんです。ヒーローは「神の補助者」を務めることがあるので、悪魔に狙われるんですよ。坂本龍馬が早死にしたのと同じです。彼もあまりに若くして亡くなったでしょう。私が死んだのと同じ年です。私たちは毎年、何歳のときも、いつの時期にも、命を落とすかどうかの瀬戸際にあるんです。

　もちろん、私たちの心は「不惜身命」（注）ですよ。古い時代を壊す「破壊者」ですからね。だから、古い時代を守ろうとしている人たちに殺されることもあります。悪魔が彼らに力を貸す場合だってあります。私は天から降りたヒーローだったけど、中国の新たなレガシー（遺産）

（注）仏教用語で、「身も命も惜しまない」ということ。

159

Chinese new legacy, I mean the hope of the Chinese people.

It is the real meaning of my young death. So, I died too young. [*Points to Wada.*] If you want to get married in the near future [*smiles while doing the eyebrow flash*], I will be waiting.

Wada [*Laughs.*]

Bruce Lee's mission as a destroyer of the old age

Sakai Now, you said "from Heaven."

Bruce Lee Yeah, of course, of course, hero of God.

Sakai Where do you live? Where are you? Now, another world, in Heaven?

Bruce Lee My living room is very small, so I don't

を、つまり中国人の希望を潰してやろうと思ってる悪魔もいるということですよ。

これが、私が早死にした真相です。だから、若すぎる死だったんです。（和田を指差して）もし君が、近いうちに結婚したくなったら（意味ありげに眉を動かして微笑みながら）待ってるからね。

和田　（笑）

古い時代の破壊者としての使命

酒井　今、「天から」とおっしゃいましたが。

ブルース・リー　そう、当然でしょう、「神のヒーロー」ですから。

酒井　どこにお住まいですか。どこにおられますか。現在、あの世の、天国にいらっしゃいますか。

ブルース・リー　私の〝リビング〟はすごく狭いんで、

161

5 Bruce Lee Reveals His Past Life, the Truth of His Death, and the Mission of His Soul

know correctly. Your living room is very huge. But I'm a friend of Ryoma Sakamoto, you know? That's enough explanation for you.

Sakai Same dimension*?

Bruce Lee Ah, no, no. Sometimes, we are friends.

Sakai Friends? Do you know other friends?

Bruce Lee [*Points to Ryoma as if he is behind Bruce Lee.*] A destroyer of the Edo period.

Sakai A destroyer, yeah, yeah.

---

* According to Happy Science, the Spirit World is divided into dimensions from four to nine in accordance to the levels of enlightenment. The lower part of the fourth dimension is Hell, the dimensions above the fifth are Heaven. Those with good hearts reside in the fifth dimension, leaders and experts in the sixth, angels in the seventh, great angels in the eight, and saviors in the ninth dimension. Refer to *The Laws of the Sun* (New York: IRH Press, 2013) and *The Nine Dimensions* (New York: IRH Press, 2012).

162

5　ブルース・リーが明かす「過去世、死の真相、魂の使命」

よくわからない。君たちの〝リビング〟はすごく広いね。ただ、坂本龍馬とは友だちですから。それを言えば十分でしょう、君たちへの説明としては。

酒井　同じ次元（注）ですか。

ブルース・リー　ああ、いやいや、友だちづき合いする「こともある」。

酒井　友だちであると。ほかにはどんな友だちがいらっしゃいますか。

ブルース・リー　（そこにいない龍馬を指差すようにして）江戸時代の破壊者だから。

酒井　破壊者ですか。なるほど。

　（注）幸福の科学では、霊界が多次元世界になっていて、心の段階に応じて、四次元から九次元まで分かれていることを明らかにしている。四次元の下部に地獄があり、五次元以上の世界が天国と言われる。五次元には善人、六次元には各界の指導者や専門家、七次元には天使、八次元には大天使、九次元には救世主が住んでいる。『太陽の法』『永遠の法』（大川隆法著・幸福の科学出版刊）参照。

163

Bruce Lee I'm a destroyer of the Chinese age of slavery.

Sakai Ah, OK.

Isono So, you destroy the old age and create a new one.

Bruce Lee Yeah, and I want to be a bridge between China and Japan, China and Hong Kong, and Hong Kong and the U.S.A., Europe, and other Asian countries. I hope so. I hope so.

Isono This is the last question from me. Could you give a message to the people of China and the world?

Bruce Lee Learn kung fu and study Happy Science.

Isono That's all?

5 ブルース・リーが明かす「過去世、死の真相、魂の使命」

ブルース・リー　私のほうは、中国の奴隷的時代の破壊者だから。

酒井　ああ、はい。

磯野　つまり、あなたは古い時代を壊して、新しい時代を創るわけですね。

ブルース・リー　そうです。そして、中国と日本、中国と香港、香港とアメリカ、ヨーロッパ、その他のアジア諸国との架け橋になりたいと思っています。それが私の願いです。そう願っています。

磯野　私からの最後の質問です。中国と世界の人々に向けてメッセージをお願いできますでしょうか。

ブルース・リー　カンフーを習うことです。そして、幸福の科学を学んでください。

磯野　以上でよろしいですか。

165

Bruce Lee That's all.

Isono OK, thank you very much.

Bruce Lee Is it OK? [*Takes a Jeet Kune Do stance.*] Do you need my new action? [*While moving both hands.*] Acho, acho! Ohh! Voice is a power! You know? You must invent a new voice. Mr. Okawa should stand at Tokyo Dome and should say, "[*Takes a stance.*] Acho!! [*As if pointing at the enemy.*] Chinese, I will punish you! Change your mind. Acho!" He should say so.

Sakai What is the meaning of "acho"?

Bruce Lee Acho means the Voice of God. Uh-huh.

Isono What does it mean?

Bruce Lee Umm, "I will destroy you."

5 ブルース・リーが明かす「過去世、死の真相、魂の使命」

ブルース・リー　以上です。

磯野　はい、ありがとうございました。

ブルース・リー　もういいの？（截拳道のような構えをして）何か新しいアクションでもお見せしますか。（両手を動かしながら）アチョー、アチョー！ オー！ 声は力である！ わかります？ 君たちも「新しい声」を発明しないと。大川さんは東京ドームに立って、こう言うといい。「（ポーズと共に）アチョー!!（敵を指差す姿勢で）中国人民よ、汝らに罰を下す！ 心を入れ替えよ。アチョー！」 そう言うといいですよ。

酒井　「アチョー」とはどういう意味ですか。

ブルース・リー　アチョーとは「神の声」です。そう。

磯野　どういう意味ですか。

ブルース・リー　ああ、「お前を滅ぼす」。

167

5 Bruce Lee Reveals His Past Life, the Truth of His Death, and the Mission of His Soul

Isono "Destroy, punish you"?

Bruce Lee "Punish you."

Isono I see.

Sakai Thank you.

Bruce Lee Is it OK?

Sakai It's OK.

Bruce Lee Is it enough? You enjoyed?

Isono Very much.

Bruce Lee Enjoyed? OK. You are a good man.

Interviewers Yes, thank you very much.

磯野　「滅ぼし、罰する」と。

ブルース・リー　「罰を下す」。

磯野　なるほど。

酒井　ありがとうございました。

ブルース・リー　もういいの？

酒井　大丈夫です。

ブルース・リー　十分かな。楽しんでくれた？

磯野　とても。

ブルース・リー　楽しんでくれた？　良かった。君はいい
人だね。

質問者一同　はい、ありがとうございました。

Bruce Lee Bye-bye.

After the spiritual interview

Ryuho Okawa [*Claps three times.*] Ah, funny guy. Bruce Lee was "the Bruce Lee." Not less than Bruce Lee, not more than Bruce Lee.

He was a hero, but not the Chinese hero only. He was a citizen of the United States and he has a lot of fans in Japan. He has influence, a lot of influence all over the world. I think so. I hope so.

Thank you, Bruce Lee.

Interviewers Thank you very much, Master Okawa.

5　ブルース・リーが明かす「過去世、死の真相、魂の使命」

ブルース・リー　バイバイ。

霊言を終えて

大川隆法　（三度、手を叩く）ああ、面白い人でしたね。「ブルース・リーはブルース・リー」でした。ブルース・リー以下でも以上でもなかったですね。

　彼はヒーローでしたが、中国のヒーローにとどまらず、米国市民でしたし、日本にも数多くのファンがいます。影響力のある人です。全世界的に大きな影響力のある人だと思いますし、そうであることを願っています。

　ブルース・リーよ、ありがとうございました。

質問者一同　総裁先生、まことにありがとうございました。

『ブルース・リーの霊言』大川隆法著作関連書籍

『神秘の法』（幸福の科学出版刊）
『太陽の法』（同上）
『永遠の法』（同上）
『老子の幸福論』（同上）
『中国民主化運動の旗手 劉暁波の霊言』（同上）
『日本よ、国家たれ！ 元台湾総統 李登輝守護霊
魂のメッセージ』（同上）

ブルース・リーの霊言
――ドラゴンの復活――

2017 年 11 月 24 日　初版第 1 刷

著　者　　大　川　隆　法

発行所　　幸福の科学出版株式会社

〒107-0052 東京都港区赤坂 2 丁目 10 番 14 号
TEL(03) 5573-7700
http://www.irhpress.co.jp/

印刷・製本　株式会社 堀内印刷所

落丁・乱丁本はおとりかえいたします
©Ryuho Okawa 2017. Printed in Japan. 検印省略
ISBN 978-4-86395-953-8 C0074
カバー Photo：prapann／Shutterstock.com
本文 Photo：Photo12／oneinchpunch／Shutterstock.com／
Grzegorz Czapski／Shutterstock.com

大川隆法 霊言シリーズ・老荘思想の真髄

老子の幸福論

「タオ（道）」の思想の本質とは？ そして、唯物論に染まった「現代中国を救う道」とは？ 2500年の時をへて、老子から現代人へのメッセージ。

1,500円

公開霊言
老子の復活・荘子の本心
中国が生んだ神秘思想の源流を探る

中国の神秘思想のルーツ──老子と荘子が、欧米と張り合って苦しんでいる現代の中国人に語った、自由と平和へのメッセージ。

1,400円

荘子の人生論

荘子が考える「自由」とは？「幸福」とは？「美」とは？ また、現代中国をどう見ているのか？ 古代中国の生んだ奇才が語る、奔放の人生論。

1,500円

幸福の科学出版

大川隆法 霊言シリーズ・中国の未来を考える

徳のリーダーシップとは何か
三国志の英雄・劉備玄徳は語る

三国志で圧倒的な人気を誇る劉備玄徳が、ついに復活！ 希代の英雄が語る珠玉の「リーダー学」と「組織論」。その真実の素顔と人心掌握の極意とは？

2,000円

秦の始皇帝の霊言
2100 中国・世界帝国への戦略

ヨーロッパ、中東、インド、ロシアも支配下に!? 緊迫する北朝鮮危機のなか、次の覇権国家を目指す中国の野望に、世界はどう立ち向かうべきか。

1,400円

中国民主化運動の旗手
劉暁波の霊言
自由への革命、その火は消えず

ノーベル平和賞受賞の民主活動家が、死後8日目に復活メッセージ。天安門事件の人権弾圧に立ち会った劉氏が後世に託す、中国民主化への熱き思いとは。

1,400円

※表示価格は本体価格（税別）です。

大川隆法著作シリーズ・最新刊

嫁の心得
山内一豊の妻に学ぶ
さげまん妻にならないための6つのヒント

賢い女性は、夫も家族も自分も幸せにできる。結婚、子育て、嫁姑問題、価値観の違い──。学校や家庭では教わらない「良妻賢母」になる方法とは。

1,500円

渡部昇一 死後の生活を語る
霊になって半年の衝撃レポート

渡部昇一氏の霊が語るリアルな霊界の様子。地上と異なる「時間」「空間」、そして「価値観」──。あの世を信じたほうが、人は幸せになれる!

1,400円

マイティ・ソーとオーディンの
北欧神話を霊査する

「正義」と「英雄」の時代が再びやってくる──。巨人族との戦い、魔術と科学、宇宙間移動など、北欧神話の神々が語る「失われた古代文明」の真実。

1,400円

幸福の科学出版

大川隆法「法シリーズ」・最新刊

伝道の法
人生の「真実」に目覚める時

法シリーズ第23作

人生の悩みや苦しみは
どうしたら解決できるのか。
世界の争いや憎しみは
どうしたらなくなるのか。
ここに、ほんとうの「答え」がある。

2,000円

第1章 心の時代を生きる　　　　　── 人生を黄金に変える「心の力」
第2章 魅力ある人となるためには── 批判する人をもファンに変える力
第3章 人類幸福化の原点　　　── 宗教心、信仰心は、なぜ大事なのか
第4章 時代を変える奇跡の力
　　　　　　　　　　　── 危機の時代を乗り越える「宗教」と「政治」
第5章 慈悲の力に目覚めるためには
　　　　　　　　　　　── 一人でも多くの人に愛の心を届けたい
第6章 信じられる世界へ── あなたにも、世界を幸福に変える「光」がある

※表示価格は本体価格(税別)です。

幸福の科学グループのご案内

宗教、教育、政治、出版などの活動を通じて、地球的ユートピアの実現を目指しています。

幸福の科学

1986年に立宗。信仰の対象は、地球系霊団の最高大霊、主エル・カンターレ。世界100カ国以上の国々に信者を持ち、全人類救済という尊い使命のもと、信者は、「愛」と「悟り」と「ユートピア建設」の教えの実践、伝道に励んでいます。

（2017年11月現在）

愛　幸福の科学の「愛」とは、与える愛です。これは、仏教の慈悲や布施の精神と同じことです。信者は、仏法真理をお伝えすることを通して、多くの方に幸福な人生を送っていただくための活動に励んでいます。

悟り　「悟り」とは、自らが仏の子であることを知るということです。教学や精神統一によって心を磨き、智慧を得て悩みを解決すると共に、天使・菩薩の境地を目指し、より多くの人を救える力を身につけていきます。

ユートピア建設　私たち人間は、地上に理想世界を建設するという尊い使命を持って生まれてきています。社会の悪を押しとどめ、善を推し進めるために、信者はさまざまな活動に積極的に参加しています。

国内外の世界で貧困や災害、心の病で苦しんでいる人々に対しては、現地メンバーや支援団体と連携して、物心両面にわたり、あらゆる手段で手を差し伸べています。

年間約3万人の自殺者を減らすため、全国各地で街頭キャンペーンを展開しています。

公式サイト **www.withyou-hs.net**

ヘレン・ケラーを理想として活動する、ハンディキャップを持つ方とボランティアの会です。視聴覚障害者、肢体不自由な方々に仏法真理を学んでいただくための、さまざまなサポートをしています。

公式サイト **www.helen-hs.net**

入会のご案内

幸福の科学では、大川隆法総裁が説く仏法真理をもとに、「どうすれば幸福になれるのか、また、他の人を幸福にできるのか」を学び、実践しています。

仏法真理を学んでみたい方へ

大川隆法総裁の教えを信じ、学ぼうとする方なら、どなたでも入会できます。入会された方には、『入会版「正心法語」』が授与されます。

信仰をさらに深めたい方へ

仏弟子としてさらに信仰を深めたい方は、仏・法・僧の三宝への帰依を誓う「三帰誓願式」を受けることができます。三帰誓願者には、『仏説・正心法語』『祈願文①』『祈願文②』『エル・カンターレへの祈り』が授与されます。

幸福の科学 サービスセンター
TEL 03-5793-1727

受付時間/
火～金:10～20時
土・日祝10～18時

幸福の科学 公式サイト
happy-science.jp

幸福の科学グループの教育・人材養成事業

教育 ハッピー・サイエンス・ユニバーシティ
Happy Science University

ハッピー・サイエンス・ユニバーシティとは

ハッピー・サイエンス・ユニバーシティ(HSU)は、大川隆法総裁が設立された
「現代の松下村塾」であり、「日本発の本格私学」です。
建学の精神として「幸福の探究と新文明の創造」を掲げ、
チャレンジ精神にあふれ、新時代を切り拓く人材の輩出を目指します。

学部のご案内

人間幸福学部

人間学を学び、新時代を切り拓くリーダーとなる

経営成功学部

企業や国家の繁栄を実現する、起業家精神あふれる人材となる

未来産業学部

新文明の源流を創造するチャレンジャーとなる

未来創造学部

時代を変え、未来を創る主役となる

政治家やジャーナリスト、ライター、俳優・タレントなどのスター、映画監督・脚本家などのクリエーター人材を育てます。4年制と短期特進課程があります。

・**4年制**
1年次は長生キャンパスで授業を行い、2年次以降は東京キャンパスで授業を行います。

・**短期特進課程(2年制)**
1年次・2年次ともに東京キャンパスで授業を行います。

HSU未来創造・東京キャンパス
〒136-0076
東京都江東区南砂2-6-5
TEL 03-3699-7707

HSU長生キャンパス
〒299-4325
千葉県長生郡長生村一松丙 4427-1
TEL 0475-32-7770

幸福の科学グループの教育・人材養成事業

学校法人 幸福の科学学園

学校法人 幸福の科学学園は、幸福の科学の教育理念のもとにつくられた教育機関です。人間にとって最も大切な宗教教育の導入を通じて精神性を高めながら、ユートピア建設に貢献する人材輩出を目指しています。

幸福の科学学園

中学校・高等学校（那須本校）
2010年4月開校・栃木県那須郡（男女共学・全寮制）
TEL 0287-75-7777
公式サイト **happy-science.ac.jp**

関西中学校・高等学校（関西校）
2013年4月開校・滋賀県大津市（男女共学・寮及び通学）
TEL 077-573-7774
公式サイト **kansai.happy-science.ac.jp**

仏法真理塾「サクセスNo.1」 **TEL 03-5750-0747**（東京本校）
小・中・高校生が、信仰教育を基礎にしながら、「勉強も『心の修行』」と考えて学んでいます。

不登校児支援スクール「ネバー・マインド」 **TEL 03-5750-1741**
心の面からのアプローチを重視して、不登校の子供たちを支援しています。
また、障害児支援の「**ユー・アー・エンゼル！**」運動も行っています。

エンゼルプランV **TEL 03-5750-0757**
幼少時からの心の教育を大切にして、信仰をベースにした幼児教育を行っています。

シニア・プラン21 **TEL 03-6384-0778**
希望に満ちた生涯現役人生のために、年齢を問わず、多くの方が学んでいます。

NPO活動支援

学校からのいじめ追放を目指し、さまざまな社会提言をしています。また、各地でのシンポジウムや学校への啓発ポスター掲示等に取り組む一般財団法人「いじめから子供を守ろうネットワーク」を支援しています。

ブログ **blog.mamoro.org**
公式サイト **mamoro.org**
相談窓口 **TEL.03-5719-2170**

幸福の科学グループ事業

政治

幸福実現党 釈量子サイト
shaku-ryoko.net

Twitter
釈量子@shakuryoko
で検索

党の機関紙
「幸福実現NEWS」

幸福実現党

内憂外患（ないゆうがいかん）の国難に立ち向かうべく、2009年5月に幸福実現党を立党しました。創立者である大川隆法党総裁の精神的指導のもと、宗教だけでは解決できない問題に取り組み、幸福を具体化するための力になっています。

 幸福実現党 党員募集中

あなたも幸福を実現する政治に参画しませんか。

○ 幸福実現党の理念と綱領、政策に賛同する18歳以上の方なら、どなたでも参加いただけます。
○ 党費：正党員（年額5千円［学生 年額2千円］）、特別党員（年額10万円以上）、家族党員（年額2千円）
○ 党員資格は党費を入金された日から1年間です。
○ 正党員、特別党員の皆様には機関紙「幸福実現NEWS（党員版）」が送付されます。

＊申込書は、下記、幸福実現党公式サイトでダウンロードできます。
住所：〒107-0052　東京都港区赤坂2-10-8 6階 幸福実現党本部

TEL 03-6441-0754　FAX 03-6441-0764
公式サイト　hr-party.jp　若者向け政治サイト　truthyouth.jp

幸福の科学グループ事業

幸福の科学出版

出版メディア事業

大川隆法総裁の仏法真理の書を中心に、ビジネス、自己啓発、小説など、さまざまなジャンルの書籍・雑誌を出版しています。他にも、映画事業、文学・学術発展のための振興事業、テレビ・ラジオ番組の提供など、幸福の科学文化を広げる事業を行っています。

アー・ユー・ハッピー？
are-you-happy.com

ザ・リバティ
the-liberty.com

 ザ・ファクト
マスコミが報道しない「事実」を世界に伝えるネット・オピニオン番組

Youtubeにて随時好評配信中！

ザ・ファクト　検索

幸福の科学出版
TEL 03-5573-7700
公式サイト irhpress.co.jp

ニュースター・プロダクション

芸能文化事業

「新時代の"美しさ"」を創造する芸能プロダクションです。2016年3月に映画「天使に"アイム・ファイン"」を、2017年5月には映画「君のまなざし」を公開しています。

公式サイト **newstarpro.co.jp**

ARI Production
（アリプロダクション）

タレント一人ひとりの個性や魅力を引き出し、「新時代を創造するエンターテインメント」をコンセプトに、世の中に精神的価値のある作品を提供していく芸能プロダクションです。

公式サイト **aripro.co.jp**

大川隆法　講演会のご案内

大川隆法総裁の講演会が全国各地で開催されています。
講演のなかでは、毎回、「世界教師」としての立場から、幸福な人生を生きるための心の教えをはじめ、世界各地で起きている宗教対立、紛争、国際政治や経済といった時事問題にする指針など、日本と世界がさらなる繁栄の未来を実現するための道筋が示されています

8月2日 東京ドーム「人類の選択」

5月14日 ロームシアター京都「永遠なるものを求めて」

2月11日 大分別府ビーコンプラザ・コンベンションホール「信じる力」

4月23日 高知県立県民体育館「人生を深く生き」

1月9日 パシフィコ横浜「未来への扉」

講演会には、どなたでもご参加いただけます。
最新の講演会の開催情報はこちらへ。　⇒

大川隆法総裁公式サイト
https://ryuho-okawa.org